The Zodiac Recipe

Dr. Jacquelyn Wiersma

OZARK
MOUNTAIN
PUBLISHING

For permission, serialization, condensation, adaptions, or for our catalog of other publications, write to Ozark Mountain Publishing, Inc., P.O. box 754, Huntsville, AR 72740, ATTN: Permissions Department.

Library of Congress Cataloging-in-Publication Data

Wiersma, Jacquelyn – 1981

The Zodiac Recipe by Jacquelyn Wiersma

A simple and fun reference guide that offers up delicious self-insight options from historical and modern tools such as astrology, numerology, personality profiles and more.

1. Astrology 2. Compatibility 3. Celebrities 4. Metaphysics

I. Wiersma, Jacquelyn, 1981   II. Astrology & Compatibility III. Title

Library of Congress Catalog Card Number: 2014960252

ISBN: 9781940265186

Cover Design: noir33.com

Book set in: Bell MT, Andalus

Book Design: Tab Pillar

Published by:

OZARK
MOUNTAIN
PUBLISHING

PO Box 754

Huntsville, AR 72740

800-935-0045 or 479-738-2348 fax: 479-738-2448

WWW.OZARKMT.COM

Printed in the United States of America

Endorsements

A simple and fun reference guide that offers up delicious self-insight options from historical and modern tools such as astrology, numerology, personality profiles and more. I love all the compatibility charts! The text spells out the details and the reference charts make it super easy to figure out who you are most compatible with—and who you're not! You'll have a new perspective on why you get along with some people and not others—and you'll have a lot of fun doing it!

~ Paula Renaye, CPC, CECP, RMT, QHHT, CEHT
(DOB: August 4; LEO)
Intuitive Coach and Energetic Clearing Facilitator
Author, Living the Life You Love: The No-Nonsense Guide to
Total Transformation
www.PaulaRenaye.com

In The Zodiac Recipe, Dr. Jacquelyn Wiersma provides a fascinating discourse on how astrology can help us understand why we are naturally attracted to some people and repulsed by others. The author explains that everyone's personality, emotions, outward demeanor, and love style, are impacted by the date and time of their birth (which determines their SUN, MOON, and ASCENDANT signs, among other things) and these factors will influence our choices for friends and mates. With wisdom and humor, Dr. Wiersma illustrates how this information can help us better understand our partners, our friends, and ourselves, so that we can focus on the things that bring us closer to the people we care about while avoiding those areas where conflicts may lurk. And for those people seeking a new relationship, this book is an easy-to-follow guide on finding a compatible mate. The Zodiac Recipe is intriguing and fun to read as it dishes up food for thought that will be savored by readers of all ages.

~ Garnet Schulhauser
(DOB: March 7, 1951; Cupar, Saskatchewan, Canada;
unknown time; PISCES/PISCES)
Author of Dancing on a Stamp

Dr. Wiersma's book, The Zodiac Recipe, is a fun and informative tool to assist us in understanding ourselves as well as our relationships with others by utilizing the astrological zodiac signs. Her entertaining approach keeps the reader engaged, fascinated and excited to read more in order to recognize how the moment of our birth plays a role in our life experiences.

~ Shelly Wilson
(DOB: December 19, 1970; 4:44 pm; Leavenworth, KS;
SAGITTARIUS; VIRGO)
Intuitive Medium and Author of 28 Days to a New YOU,
Connect to the YOU Within and Journey into Consciousness
www.shellyrwilson.com

There are so many things that I love about this book, beginning with the fact that an Assistant Professor from the University of Arkansas is the author. Those of us who are interested in astrology already know that it's an important science, and Dr. Wiersma's fascinating tome heralds a new era of credibility for master and amateur astrologists, while providing her readers with an easy-to-understand and nearly effortless recipe that is certain to help us better understand ourselves and our relationships. Using Dr. Wiersma's instructions, I quickly pulled together a mini-chart for myself and my husband and the results were 100% on target with regard to our individual personalities and our relationship. I also like that she's incorporated Chinese astrology and numerology to help us discover our truest portrait. As a Scorpio sun sign (with my moon in Taurus), you know that I'm going to tell it like it is, and this book is one that I intend to give to my family and friends as a holiday gift. Whether you are currently in a relationship, or seeking to make the best match possible, the information is this book is eye-opening, exceptionally useful, and important.

~ Sherri Cortland, ND
(DOB: November 7, 1957; 12:15 a.m.; Nyack, NY;
SCORPIO; TAURUS)
Author of Windows of Opportunity, Raising our Vibrations for the
New Age, Spiritual Toolbox, and Guide Group Fridays

Table of Contents

Dedication

First and foremost, this book would not be possible without the support from two very important people who continually told me that I could write this book and that I would get it published, even when I had major doubts. So thank you to my friends Leanna Potts and Lori Kriegner for being my biggest fans! Second, I would not even have gotten into Zodiacs/Astrology if it wasn't for my friend, Sunam – we had such a beautiful friendship that I often miss, but for some reason, that darn Cancer-Aquarius incompatibility got in our way. Our friendship breakup is ultimately what led me to Zodiacs to help me realize why we were incompatible. I think we worked for so long because of my Pisces cusp; however, we are just very different. But I learned so much from our friendship and am grateful you were in my life, even if for a short time. Lastly, thank you to my friends and family for listening to me rant endlessly about Zodiacs/Astrology for the past 4 years, as I'm sure it was quite annoying! I'm so glad my mom is a Scorpio/Aquarius and that we are compatible, as she's one of my best friends. And I'm so glad I finally met my compatible partner in my husband Wade (an Aquarius as well), who at first thought I was crazy for all this nonsense talk, but has nonetheless been supportive and loving throughout this process.

Foreword

Astrology: In the West, astrology most often consists of a system of horoscopes that claim to predict aspects of an individual's personality or life history based on the positions of the sun, moon, and other planetary objects at the time of their birth.

So what possessed me to write a book about astrology and zodiac signs? Honestly, I can say that it has a lot to do with human curiosity about the way we relate to one another. For example, have you ever wondered why are we attracted to certain partners? Why do we get along with certain friends but not others? How come some of us are better friends with our parents or even one parent over the other? How come we like certain co-workers but can't stand other ones? This curiosity is why I became interested in astrology and zodiac signs.

Trust me when I say I am just as skeptical as the next person when it comes to astrology. I'm asked a lot why I'm so interested in this topic since I'm a scientist with a Ph.D. And yes, I am a scientist with a Ph.D., and I believe in scientific research, but that's what I've been doing for the past few years with astrology—doing my research. Granted, I can't say that there is any scientific evidence to support astrology, but I can say that my thorough researching skills have brought me to one very important conclusion: It's more than just a coincidence. I can't tell you how many people I've interacted with or people I've looked up (such as celebrity birthdays, see Chapter 5) and discovered so many interesting patterns, based on compatibilities between people. It's absolutely fascinating to me.

This isn't exactly a book that gets a lot of prestige among academics. At least the Ph.D. might give me some credit or at the very least ruin my academic reputation, right?! It's not easy to put yourself out there with some very highly controversial opinions on a subject matter like this, especially when most people believe that zodiacs are rubbish. I ask my large Family Relations class (over 250 students) at the University of Arkansas every semester two questions, and I'm still amazed by the responses:

1) "Do you believe in a soul mate?" 75% say YES; and

2) "Do you believe in zodiacs/astrology" 75% say NO.

Thus, my students (like most people) believe that there is only ONE person in the entire world for them (approximately 6.8 billion people), but yet they can't comprehend or believe that someone's birthday might, "MIGHT" have some meaning. This is odd, considering that approximately 70 million Americans read their horoscopes every day!

So one question that I've been asking myself is how is this book different from all the ones that have already been published on this subject? Well, my first thought is I have a Ph.D., and this is a very different perspective than what's been written so far. I study human relations, and this book can relate to anyone. Additionally, I've done a lot of research on this topic by reading books, online blogs, and talking to people incessantly about this topic for the past few years. I've discussed my knowledge with many believers and non-believers, and even the non-believers found it fascinating.

So I challenge each and every one of you (this is what I tell my students!): If you're a believer or non-believer of astrology, I challenge you to do either of these:

1) go to Facebook and look up all your friends' birthdays. I bet their birthdays will be very compatible with your own birthday.

2) if you don't have a Facebook account, then I challenge you to go out and do it the old fashioned way—ask them!

For some reason, I have a gift of remembering birthdays. I can't for the love of me remember someone's name, but I can remember that person's birthday. Most of my friends are Libras (compatible with my SUN sign). I've also dated a lot of Libras.

And lately, I have a weird gift of predicting someone's sun sign. I kid you not. I've encountered numerous people in the past few years, and I'll predict their signs without knowing their birthdays. I've done this with students in my classroom, friends, colleagues, and other people's accounts of their friends, and I find that I'm almost always right.

Trust me, I've thought a lot about the different relationships in my life, those I got along with and those I didn't, and I challenge you to do the same. Even if you don't believe in astrology, I think it's still interesting to discover if there is a pattern. How we think about and view the world comes from our zodiac make up. I'm almost convinced of this, but I can't prove it…just yet.

It should be no surprise to those who really know me as to why I'm so interested in this subject: my main research interest is in mate selection and development. Thus, both my dissertation and ongoing research examine why people select certain mates/partners based on alcohol consumption and how that impacts their relationships.

Selection is an evolutionary process in which selecting or choosing a mate depends on attractiveness of its traits—thus, we are attracted most often to those who are similar to ourselves. Most of my research has utilized this concept.

Plus, I'm interested in how individuals develop over time, which is very important. I believe that you don't become your true self or your true zodiac until you are mid to late 20s. Another reason why this subject matter naturally interests me is that my Sun sign is Aquarius. I once read that Aquarians are some of the most likely people to be interested in zodiacs. I was sold. ☺

Jacquelyn Wiersma, Ph.D.
(DOB: February 16, 1981 (11:55 pm);
Le Mars, IA 51031; AQUARIUS; LEO)

My zodiac recipe blog: http://zodiacrecipe.wordpress.com/

The Zodiac Recipe

From the Show Big Bang Theory

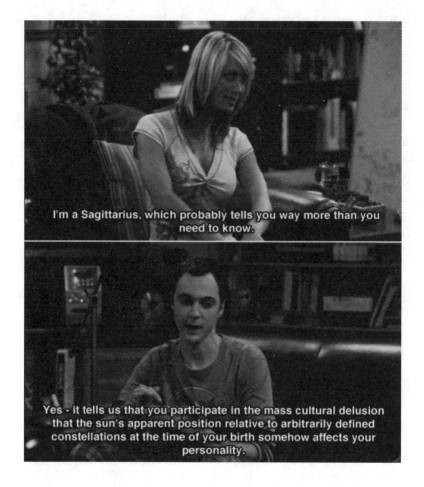

I'm a Sagittarius, which probably tells you way more than you need to know.

Yes - it tells us that you participate in the mass cultural delusion that the sun's apparent position relative to arbitrarily defined constellations at the time of your birth somehow affects your personality.

Chapter 1
Quick Background on Zodiacs

In case you don't know much about astrology and zodiac signs, I am going to spend a little time going over this. First, there are twelve zodiac signs (as you'll read in Chapter 2), which one would assume means twelve personality types, but this is misconstrued. There's a lot more to people than just their main zodiac SUN sign just like there's a lot more to a cake than just flour. For example, the full birth chart has all the essential ingredients you need to fully understand yourself and your relationships.

Zodiac signs are grouped into four essential elements which help in understanding everybody's place in the world. The zodiac elements are Fire, Earth, Air, and Water. Zodiac elements are extremely symbolic with the astrology sign that they represent and will help you gain a greater understanding of people's signs and how they behave in life. The elements are important in laying the groundwork to understanding the characteristics and personality traits of a person.

FIRE contains ARIES, LEO, and SAGITTARIUS, and these are typically the leaders and opinionated individuals of the zodiac. Never subtle and the most confident of all the signs, they are very compatible with one another and with AIR signs.

EARTH contains TAURUS, VIRGO, and CAPRICORN, and these people are very practical and grounded. I also like to add very stubborn! Talk about rocks! They are the most stable, consistent and sometimes rigid of all the signs. Once they make up their minds, like mountains they cannot be moved without huge efforts. Practical, patient, reasonable, and persistent are these people. If you want to make sure projects get done and done right, call on an EARTH people. They will stick with the project until the bitter end. Also, they are not much for spontaneity or flexibility. Not as sensitive as the WATER signs, the EARTH signs are still aware of others' needs and often want to serve others. They are very compatible with one another and with WATER signs.

1

AIR contains GEMINI, LIBRA, and AQUARIUS and are the communicators of the zodiac, ruled by their rational thinking. Always moving and changing. Just when we think we know them, poof! They change again. AIR signs are very compatible with one another and also with FIRE signs. They are not compatible with EARTH (too rigid for them) and WATER (too emotional for them).

WATER contains CANCER, SCORPIO, and PISCES and are the stereotypical feminine and emotional types of people who are ruled by their emotions. Feelings, emotions, and deep personal conversations motivate and stimulate the WATER signs. Sensitive to a fault, the WATER signs are often more concerned with others' feelings and needs than their own. You can find them at movies crying loudest and most often. Everything seems to touch them. WATER signs are most compatible with one another and with EARTH signs.

Remember:

Signs within the same element are very compatible with one another (for example, within FIRE: Aries, Leos and Sagittarians are very compatible).

There are four main categories of signs: Fire, Earth, Air, and Water, and there are three zodiacs within each of these.

Chapter 2

Your Zodiac Recipe

Ingredients:

½ Cup Sun sign
¾ Cup Moon sign
¼ Cup Ascendant sign
4 TBSP Planets
½ TSP Cusps

1/2 Cup SUN SIGN

Ok, so let's get started. First of all, most of us know our SUN sign. It's the most obvious: the day you were born. For example, I was born on February 16, thus my SUN sign is Aquarius, but I also fall into the Aquarius/Pisces Cusp (but we'll discuss that important ingredient later). The SUN sign is definitely important, like the sugar in cake, but it is not as important as people always think.

Yes, it can tell you a lot about a person, but it really only tells you about 50-60% about someone. The SUN sign represents your personality. It's not completely accurate but still important and explains why two people with the same sign may differ so greatly. Also, it's not going to tell you whether someone likes country vs. hip hop music or whether someone should play a certain sport. It's not that detailed. It's more about temperament, I believe, and more about our outside behavior that people see, such as introverted vs. extroverted, leader vs. follower, or even sensitive vs. non-sensitive. It is the broad definition of someone, not the specific characteristics.

I'll give you my interpretation quickly of each SUN sign (personality) and then followed by more thorough descriptions from my favorite website, Café Astrology (http://www.cafeastrology.com/index. html). Then you can read your SUN sign and decide how accurately it portrays you:

ARIES (March 21-April 19)

The most headstrong and opinionated people of the zodiac. When I think of a male, the stereotypical male, who's hardheaded and rough, rugged, and determined, I think of an Aries, but obviously there are female Aries, so I give similar traits to them. You may even call a female Aries the stereotypical "bitch" who doesn't back down from an argument. These people are spitfires. If they have an opinion, then you'll know about it quickly, and that is where they come from: FIRE!

Aries is the first sign of the zodiac, and Aries natives are the first to start—and the first to finish—whatever they set out to do. Aries is an active, energetic sign, so these individuals are often direct, straightforward, and uncomplicated. They expect the same from others, and are baffled when they don't always get it. Those born in Aries enjoy a challenge and are happiest when their lives are moving forward and active. There's a childlike quality to all Aries people, and it's often quite charming.

It had long since come to my attention that people of accomplishment rarely sat back and let things happen to them. They went out and happened to things.

Eleanor Furneaux Smith

TAURUS (April 20-May 20)

The most stubborn of all the zodiac signs. By far, when someone asks me what characterizes a Taurus, my first thought is stubbornness! They are also very traditional and intelligent. These people are very

practical and most likely to be able to handle the 9-5 job, and they won't ever end a relationship with a partner—even if they are miserable. They just never want to give up. Thus, their partners or friends have to be the ones to end the relationships. Again, these are the most stubborn. They are like their EARTH sign, grounded and immovable!

There is something very solid about Taurus natives, no matter what the rest of their charts say about them. Though they are dependable most of the time, this generally shows itself more in habit than in outright helpfulness.

Live simple, love well, and take time to smell the flowers along the way.
Mark Twain

GEMINI (May 21-June 20)

Oh boy, if you know a Gemini, then you probably can't get a word in. These people are talkers! They love to communicate, which is a quality of the AIR element. I haven't seen this with every Gemini I know, but they often say these people have two personalities (hence the two tiers or twins often portrayed in pictures). This could mean they are just crazy (multiple personalities) but also that they are the most likely to get along with almost everyone because they have more than one side to them.

With the Sun in Gemini, the urge for self-expression is strong. These natives are often just as interested in collecting information as they are in sharing it. Curious to a fault, Geminis have a finger in every pie. Gemini's are flexible and changeable people. Their ability to adapt quickly to new situations generally gains them plenty of friends and social contacts. Usually quite clever and witty, Geminis enjoy intellectual conversations, and they are easily bored if they are not getting enough mental stimulation.

There are no uninteresting things, there are only uninterested people.
Gilbert K. Chesterton

CANCER (June 21-July 22)

The main characteristic that describes this sign is emotional and moody. These people can be quick to change emotions, so you better beware! This sign is typically pictured as a crab! If you mess with  them or hurt them, don't ever expect them to forgive you, but one thing I love about these people is that they are quirky! They are some of the funniest and wittiest people in the zodiac. Also, I've read that the two most important things to Cancers are #1 family and #2 money.

Sun in Cancer natives have a strong survival instinct. They are protective of those they care about and of themselves, too. They are often quite reticent about sharing their inner selves to the rest of the world and are often caught up in reminiscence. Cancers needs roots. They resist change to an extent and concern themselves with being secure and safe in most everything they do.

Love...force it and it disappears. You cannot will love, nor even control it. You can only guide its expression. It comes or it goes according to those qualities in life that invite it or deny its presence.
David Seabury

LEO (July 23-August 20)

Who doesn't love a Leo? Seriously, most Leos are the life of the party and so outgoing, friendly, and fun! However, there are negative and positive traits to every sign, and I have met an extremely negative Leo who was hard to be around. Most Leos are known for being great leaders because people can't help but follow them since they are amazing people! A lot of Presidents (i.e., Clinton and Obama) and celebrities are Leos, and one thing is for sure—we love our celebrities in the West.

There's an unmistakably regal air to Leos. These are dignified—even noble—folks. Leos have a reputation for being conceited. Leos do feel important, but this generally takes the form of wanting to change the world in some way—to make the world a better place. They are generally motivated by affection for people and often have big dreams and plans to make people happy.

Let your enthusiasm radiate in your voice, your actions, your facial expressions, your personality, the words you use, and the thoughts you think! Nothing great was ever achieved without enthusiasm.
Ralph Waldo Emerson

VIRGO (August 21-September 20)

These people are some of the most intelligent in the zodiac, very practical and strong, and analytical. They are usually organized because they like everything a certain way.

Virgo people are generally respectable, hardworking individuals who have a love of knowledge and know-how. There's an odd combination of the intellectual and the practical in Virgo that is sometimes mistaken for coolness. In fact, Virgos are often self-effacing and shy. They'll brush off your compliments quickly and sometimes critically. Don't let that fool you; they need your respect and appreciation. In fact, the happiest Virgos are the ones who feel appreciated and useful. Add plenty of worthwhile projects to keep them busy, and Virgos can be some of the sweetest, kindest people around.

When I am working on a problem, I never think about beauty. I think only how to solve the problem. But when I have finished, if the solution is not beautiful, I know it is wrong.
Buckminster Fuller

LIBRA (September 21-October 22):

Some of my favorite people are Libras because they are just such good mediators and can see both sides to a story. They are the most diplomatic and fair people in the zodiac. And they are also extremely communicative and love to talk about everything. They often have difficulty making decisions because they are so easy-going. These are the folks that when you ask them what they want to eat or do, they say, "Oh, I don't care."

Libra natives are generally thought to be sociable, somewhat intellectual souls. They have an almost innocent way about them that makes them very approachable. Generally quite eager to cooperate, Libras spend a lot of their time trying not to rock the boat. On the fence, middle ground, middle road—these are all expressions that we can safely associate with Libra.

We can choose to throw stones, to stumble on them, to climb over them, or to build with them.

William Arthur Ward

SCORPIO (October 23-November 21)

In my opinion, these are the most confusing types of people, and not in a bad way, but in the sense that they vary so much. It's so difficult to tell who a Scorpio is. These are the most difficult for me to pinpoint. I think it's because they have the most depth of all the signs. People of this sign can fall into the extremes for they are the most passionate of all the signs. I've also read that they are the most jealous and manipulative, but I don't find that with all of the people I've met who are Scorpio. That's why it can be difficult to define them, but one thing is for sure: if you mess with them, beware of their stinger!

Scorpios are known for their intensity. They are determined folk that absolutely throw themselves into whatever they do, but getting them to commit to something is rarely an easy task. In fact, it's better not to even try to get them to do anything. Scorpios absolutely have their own mind. Their primary motivation is unlikely to be prestige, or even authority—it's real power. Their power can absolutely be of the behind the scenes variety—just as long as they have it.

Everyone has talent. What is rare is the courage to follow the talent to the dark place where it leads.

Erica Jong

SAGITTARIUS (November 22-December 21)

Some of the friendliest people of the zodiac, Sagittarians are also the most political. These people love a good debate and love to discuss politics, philosophy or controversial topics because they are usually well versed in those areas. They have strong opinions, but not as strong as their sister sign, Aries. They are good leaders but probably not as good as their other sister sign, Leo. However, they are the best at debating. One great example of a Sagittarian is Jon Stewart of the Daily Show—a true essential Sagittarian!

Restless, cheerful, and friendly, Sun in Sagittarius people are generally on the go. They have a love of freedom and a disdain for routine. Generally quite easygoing, Sagittarians make friends with people from all walks of life. They love to laugh and tease and get along well with both sexes.

If one advances confidently in the direction of his dreams, and endeavors to live the life which he has imagined, he will meet with a success unexpected in common hours.

Henry David Thoreau

CAPRICORN (December 22-January 19):

Capricorns are the hardest working people in the zodiac, hands down. They are very likely to be called workaholics. They are very practical  and hardheaded (but not as much as a Taurus) and also known to be romantic in their own ways—not the flashy type but in a more practical manner. They'll lavish a romantic partner in practical ways (do you need a new vacuum cleaner?).

Capricorn is a feet-on-the-ground, eye-on-the-prize sign. Those with Sun in Capricorn have a realistic, grounded approach to life that can be seen no matter how dreamy the rest of the birth chart suggests. These people know how to do things and get things done.

Success doesn't mean the absence of failures; it means the attainment of ultimate objectives. It means winning the war, not every battle.
Edwin C. Bliss

AQUARIUS (January 20-February 18)

This is my favorite sign (my sign!) because it encompasses me completely. Aquarians are some of the most intelligent and unique individuals in the zodiac. They love to talk about everything, hence, communicate (an AIR sign). But they are  super stubborn as well and value independence so much that it borders on insanity. They are so ruled by their rational mind that they have a difficult time being emotional or relating to people who are emotional. Thus, they have a few negative traits too! Also, I've read that Aquarians feel like aliens from another planet—they just feel out of place. They are also the most likely to be ahead of their time—very progressive individuals, humanitarians, who think differently than others.

One of the prominent characteristics of those born under the Sun sign of Aquarius is their unwillingness to follow the beaten track. With advancement and progress on their minds, they can be derisive of old and outdated ways of thinking and doing things. Aquarians need space and value personal freedom. Any attempt to box them in will likely fail. They'll happily return the favor; and they will treat people from all walks of life as equals. Equality and fairness are hallmarks of the sign. If you're quirky and different, all the better.

If a man does not keep pace with his companions, perhaps it is because he hears a different drummer. Let him step to the music he hears, however measured or far away.

Henry David Thoreau

PISCES (February 19-March 20):

Pisceans are the most sensitive people in the zodiac. Try not to hurt these people's feelings even though it may be hard to do unintentionally. Besides being overly emotional (WATER sign; fish are portrayed often in photos), they are some of the most loving and sympathetic people you'll meet, also the most adaptable of all the signs. And interestingly enough, they are most likely to be psychic! One pattern I've found is that a lot of comedians are PISCES, which surprised me (they are sensitive!), but in a way it makes sense because they are empathetic and able to know what people find to be funny in any given situation. (Example: Chelsea Handler).

As the twelfth and last sign of the zodiac, Pisces contains within itself a little experience of all the signs. This gives Pisces Suns the ability to identify with people from all walks of life and from all backgrounds in some way. These individuals are not only changeable and adaptable, they have open minds and tremendous understanding;

however, Pisces itself is often misunderstood. Pisces Suns may spend a good portion of their lives yearning for understanding and the other part in a state of divine discontent. Suffering is sometimes glamorized in the Piscean world.

Resolve to be tender with the young, compassionate with the aged, sympathetic with the striving, and tolerant with the weak and the wrong. Sometime in life you will have been all of these.

Robert Goddard

Remember:

Sun signs represent your personality, and next we will discuss probably one of the most essential ingredients in your Zodiac recipe, which is the MOON sign.

3/4 Cup MOON SIGN

Most people do not know their MOON sign, or even why the MOON sign is important. I'm here to tell you it's very, very important. The MOON represents your emotions. Remember how the SUN represents your personality? Well, the MOON encompasses your deep emotions, which explains a person even better than a SUN sign. Hence, this explains why some people do not fit their SUN sign perfectly. As stated before, the SUN explains about 50-60% of someone, whereas the MOON explains about 60-80%.

Now the MOON sign is a little more complicated: You need to use a MOON calculator to discover your own Moon sign. Here's one website, but there are countless others: (http://www.astrocal.co.uk /moonsign/moonsignmain.html) A MOON sign represents where the moon was located when you were born. So the date is important, as well as the year, location, and time of birth! All are essential ingredients, which unfortunately, not everyone knows. For example, my birth date was February 16, 1981, at 11:55 pm in Le Mars, Iowa. Side note: I was almost born on the 17th; the doctor yelled at my mother, "If you want this baby on the 16th, you better push!" So she did, and I'm much happier with a 16th birth date anyway! I'll also never forget the time because of that story.

It's unfortunate that so many people do not know their birth time. So with my time of birth, my MOON sign is LEO, which actually really surprised me at first. I don't feel like I'm anything like a LEO, but the MOON is a little different than the SUN characteristics. Remember that it's more representative of your emotions, especially in romantic relationships. Again, here are some things I've picked up from talking to people about their MOON signs. In addition here are some characteristics taken from my favorite website, Café Astrology (http://www.cafeastrology.com/index.html):

ARIES MOON

Moon in Aries people possess inner passion and fire. Emotional issues take precedence. There is simply no pussy-footing around when it comes to dealing with their feelings, and dealing with new sentiments and needs stirs up a huge desire for activity. Those with a Moon in Aries have a need for acting out and no time to waste. It is hard for them to see the long term or wait for things to happen. Instant gratification rules! Sometimes they can be quite aggressive as well, so be careful with these types unless you like that!

TAURUS MOON

Since Taurus is a practical earth sign, the placement of the Moon in this sign suggests an ability to protect themselves and their own interests. They will rarely make a move without first determining that it is safe and that there's something in it for them. Relationships with people born with this position of the Moon are often quite enduring. Many Moon in Taurus people hang onto their mates even in the face of serious conflict. Taurus is a fixed sign, so break-ups don't happen easily. Also, I've encountered numerous Taurus moon people who find gardening and cooking to be very important when they are relaxing.

GEMINI MOON

Nervousness and worry are common traits with this lunar position. An underlying restlessness is common, and many Geminis need more stimulation than others. They usually read a lot, talk a lot, and think a lot with this airy, mutable position of the Moon. When problems arise, the first instinct of Moon in Gemini natives is to talk things out. Their tendency to analyze can give them the appearance of emotional detachment. In fact, they may be especially comfortable talking about their feelings, but feeling their own feelings doesn't come as easily. Those that don't take time out to really understand their own needs may end up baffling others. Feeling misunderstood is common for these natives. The only real solution to the problem is learning to get in touch with their own feelings.

CANCER MOON

This is the most subjective position of the Moon. The Moon is at home in the sign of Cancer as the Moon is the natural ruler of the sign. Moon in Cancer natives have a large potential to be able to get in touch with the feelings and moods of others. Often they are quite wrapped up in themselves. Their memories of the past are outstanding, especially for all things emotional. Moon in Cancer people are never detached—they cling to things, their home, and people they care for. They seek out security and familiarity in all they do. They look for peace and quiet. Their attachment to all that is safe means they are a little leery of change. These peace-loving souls dislike superficiality in all of its forms. They are devoted and accommodating. One of the most delightful characteristics of Moon in Cancer people is their loony sense of humor. These people can be extraordinarily funny. Their moodiness can baffle others, but their unique outlook on life is something most people can appreciate.

LEO MOON

Moon in Leo people are not necessarily outgoing. When they feel comfortable, they do like being the center of attention. That is, they like being in the spotlight in the comfort of their own homes and with family and friends. They enjoy entertaining others and often take on the role of comic. Leos often feel a need to organize and even control their families and friends. They have an inner mission to set things right and generally like to oversee everything going on in their little circle. This is a rather creative position of the Moon. At the very least, Moon in Leo people want to create and entertain. They can be rather lazy at times and a little bossy, too. Generally though, they have a deep need to treat others fairly and justly. They are often popular folks who are valued for their integrity and strong sense of justice. Generally, it is easy to reason with them, and appealing to their well-developed sense of fairness usually works well.

VIRGO MOON

Virgos find security in the little things in life. They feel most content when they've straightened out all the details of everyday life. Many of them enjoy running errands, paying bills, and balancing the books. They take care of these things happily although some won't let on. In fact, many Virgos are quite practiced at nagging and complaining. As long as they are appreciated, however, these people will help you take care of your life, too. They are at their best when they feel useful and needed. If somebody needs help, they are generally the first to jump up and take on the task. Some of the most skeptical people are Moon in Virgos. They can't help but poke holes when faced with others' blind faith. Their criticism can be maddening, and their insistence on seeing the practical in anything emotional can be challenging, especially if you are the dreamy type. Also, they hate chaos although at times they create it!

LIBRA MOON

Moon in Libra people have a strong need for partnership. Without someone to share their lives with, they feel utterly incomplete. This is why many people with this position get involved in marriages or living-together arrangements quite young. Because this drive for harmony, peace, and sharing is so powerful, Libras are apt to do a lot of conceding. They are sympathetic and concerned for others, enjoy socializing, and revel in a good debate. Mental rapport with others is especially important to them.

SCORPIO MOON

While others may find security and comfort in material things, Moon in Scorpio people seek out emotional intensity. No matter what, there is something very intense about Scorpios. They are diggers when it comes to the world of emotion—they can see beyond facades and cut right to the core of a person. This ability to see what isn't obvious to the rest of the world can be intimidating to others or wildly attractive, depending on the audience. Moon in Scorpio people often have a strong fear of betrayal. They seek out commitment and feel the need for a partner to give up something for them. Some will put the people they love through a series of tests, though not always consciously. Their apparent suspicion can be trying for the people who love them. However, once committed, Moon in Scorpio people can be the most loyal and protective partners around. Even the shy ones have enormous presence. Their lives are emotion-driven, yet many Moon in Scorpio natives spend a lot of time controlling and mastering their emotions. Their intuition is enormous although it is sometimes self-serving. Moon in Scorpio people radiate strength. Another thing that is randomly true of Scorpio moon people is their of love hot showers, extremely hot showers.

SAGITTARIUS MOON

More than anything, Sagittarians have a need for personal freedom and space. They are extraordinarily happy and easygoing folks, as long as they don't feel caged in or cooped up. Sagittarians have a simultaneous need for activity. Meeting new people, going out in the world, and travel are all important to their sense of well-being. They love open spaces and rooms with an expansive, bright environment. Many people with this position are outdoorsy types. At the very least, they have a great love for friendly competition. Random—but many of them love horses.

CAPRICORN MOON

Being useful and productive are basic needs for Capricorns. Because they generally keep their emotions under check, Moon in Capricorn people come across as competent people. However turbulent their emotions may be under the surface, Capricorns keep cool-headed— and they come across as steady and reliable people. Messy emotions and leaky souls are a bit frightening for most with this position of the Moon. Truth is, they can have plenty of mood swings and some dark emotions now and again. They are often quite hard on themselves and would benefit from letting their guard down once in a while. They quickly garner reputations of being mountains of strength, and they easily hide their sensitivity behind a sarcastic manner.

AQUARIUS MOON

These individuals are lifetime students of human nature, loving to analyze why people do what they do. This often stems from a detached—even shy—personality, especially in youth. Whether due to character or conditioning, Moon in Aquarius people often grow up feeling different. Although rather sociable, they are often loners at heart. Many have strong egos or at least powerful defense mechanisms, and most Moon in Aquarians will do their best to be the most unique and unusual person they can be. Their inner feeling of loneliness—that they don't quite fit in—puts them on the outside, looking in. They often pride themselves on being cool-headed, detached, and above what they consider the more base emotions. In the process, they can end up alienating others—and themselves. They make unusual and endlessly interesting people to be around. Life just wouldn't be the same without Aquarians unusual spin on the world and the people in it!

PISCES MOON

Generally considered soft-hearted and sweet, Pisceans care about others and are easily touched by human suffering. This tendency gains them the reputation as suckers for sob stories. Although this may sometimes be true, in their lifetimes many Pisceans learn how to discern between sincerity and manipulation. Still, they definitely do have plenty of soft corners. They have an ability to empathize even in the absence of experience which gives them an open mind and heart. Most long to express this through writing, music (both listening and making), poetry, and art—in fact, the happiest people with this position do just that. Pisces Moon individuals believe; and let's face it, the world needs Piscean leaps of faith.

Remember:

Moon signs represent your emotions or how you are in your relationships, and thus, are extremely important that these be compatible in your romantic relationships, an essential ingredient. Next, we'll discuss Ascendant signs, which are the most difficult for people to figure out.

1/4 Cup ASCENDANT SIGN

The ASCENDANT sign is probably the most abstract of all the elements in understanding one's birth chart and the most difficult to figure out. The ASCENDANT sign (or rising sun as some call it) is characterized by how you come across to others, your outward demeanor. As Café Astrology defines it, "it is the first impression we make on others in a personal rather than professional sense. It represents our physical appearance, our physical bodies and overall health and often is referred to as the mask we wear." It is an extremely important part of our recipe to remember when we are trying to understand people, but again, it is difficult to decipher if you don't have a birth chart calculator. The best one I've encountered is located here at Café Astrology: (http://www.cafeastrology. com /ascendant. html). But the most important thing about the ASCENDANT sign is that you must know the time of birth. If you don't have that information, then you won't be able to figure it out. My ASCENDANT sign is Scorpio when you plug all my information into this website. Go and figure yours out! Here's a brief capture of all the ASCENDANT sign meanings:

ARIES

People with Aries Ascendants are direct and quick. Their first instinct is to do rather than to think. Planning ahead? Forget it. Aries-rising simply charges forward without much ado.

TAURUS

Slow, steady, and capable are adjectives that we can safely attach to individuals born with a Taurus Ascendant. These natives have tremendous stamina and staying power. They're often quite loyal to those they care about. Although they generally don't come on strong, they have a personal presence, and they radiate stability.

GEMINI

Those born with Gemini rising see the world as a place to learn. They are curious about the people around them and mostly interested in moving about in their social circles.

CANCER

These people come across as gentle creatures. There's something familiar about them—they're the guy or gal next door. When they enter a room, they don't walk in with a splash. Instead, they move to the sides and weave their way inwards. These people have a familiar feel to them. Because they are rather sensitive to their environment, they can get flustered easily, especially in public.

LEO

Leo rising people cannot help but be noticed. They radiate a special energy and magnetism that gets others' attention. Sometimes it's because they are loud people who pay a lot of attention to their personal appearance (especially their hair!); other times it's due to a regal manner that simply demands interest from others.

VIRGO

Generally, there is an unmistakable intelligent and reserved aura about Virgo rising individuals. These are actually somewhat shy people who need time to analyze things around them before they warm up to both situations and people. This quality can be received exactly as that, or it can be received as rather stand-offish.

LIBRA

Everybody seems to like Libra Ascendant natives. They just come across as nice, pleasant, and fair. Look a little closer at their lives, and these nice people may have had quite a few problems in their relationships. Some of them have had a string of relationships, and it can be hard to imagine why. These natives attract others to them effortlessly. Besides, they simply don't know what to do with themselves without a significant other.

SCORPIO

Scorpio Ascendant people have a lot of presence. There is something about them that tells the world that they are not to be pushed around. Their manner commands respect, and in some cases, fear. Scorpio rising people can be quiet or loud, but they always seem powerful and determined. You either love or hate Scorpio rising people—they are rarely people who go through life unnoticed. In fact, some of them are confused when faced with the fact that they get such strong reactions from others. They seem to look right through people, seeing through superficiality.

SAGITTARIUS

The world is filled with adventure, new things to experience and most of all, hope, with this Ascendant. There is an unmistakable faith and enthusiasm with Sagittarius rising people. Grand schemes, big promises, and a willingness to explore and experiment are themes although follow-through is not a strong characteristic of Sagittarius.

CAPRICORN

There's a seriousness to Capricorn rising people that is unmistakable. Even when they're joking around, it's the deadpan variety. In fact, plenty of very humorous people have Capricorn Ascendants. It's all in the timing—and the fact that they don't giggle before the joke is over. Capricorn Ascendant people project competence. They simply ooze it. They're generally very image-conscious people—the clothes they wear and their manner are a big deal to them. They want to appear successful, and they generally succeed.

AQUARIUS

How unique and original Aquarius rising natives come across! These individuals are just that—individuals—and they won't let you forget that fact. Often turned to for advice, these natives possess intellectual poise and savvy. They often are curious and quite learned in both science and metaphysics—anything that involves advancement of the human race holds much appeal.

PISCES

Go with the flow seems to be a Pisces rising motto. They move about the world in a vaguely directionless, gentle manner. They come across as artists and lovers of peace; but their open minds and hearts can give them a chameleon-like persona. Others are not always sure who they'll meet from one day to the next with a Pisces rising person.

Although often quiet and shy, another day may find them talkative and passionate. They are hugely impressionable, have a dreamy disposition, and project a soft-hearted personality. Pisces-rising individuals see the world the way they want to see it at any given time, so objectivity is not necessarily a strong point. Neither is decision-making!

Remember:

Ascendant signs are how you represent yourself to the world, but are based on the time of your birth, which can be difficult to assess because a lot of people are not aware of that small detail. Go find your birth certificate! Next, we'll discuss the planets in our birth chart, or the more important ones in my opinion.

4 TBSP PLANETS

I always feel like this is where I start sounding really crazy, and I start getting weird looks when I discuss planets with people! First of all, there are a bundle of planets that are important in the birth chart, but I'm going to focus only on three of them, the more essential ones in my opinion. Obviously, if you are interested in the other ones, you should definitely read up on them, and Café Astrology does an excellent job of breaking down information on each planet. Those planets include Mercury (your communication with others), Venus (your love style), Mars (your aggressive side), Jupiter (your generosity and tolerance of others), Saturn (your limitations and fears), Uranus (your future), Neptune (your intuition, spirituality), and Pluto (your truths, deeper meaning). Notice: Earth is missing. Well, that's because it encompasses so much, such as our element, whether we are FIRE, EARTH, AIR, or WATER.

I'm only going to focus on MERCURY, VENUS and MARS for now. These three planets are ones that I always look for in understanding someone. Understanding these always seems to be able to tell you a lot about a person. I haven't found as much use for the others, as they are a lot more general, but again, this is just my opinion.

MERCURY

MERCURY not only rules communication, it represents coordination. It can represent whether we are flowery in our speech and/or written words, concise in our choice of words, or business-like even in our personal communications. How do we express and convey our thoughts? How do we approach others and information in order to learn and exchange ideas? On a personal level, look to Mercury in the chart to reveal how individuals get their point across, how they study, and how they process information. Mercury shows an individual's style of communication. Mercury, the messenger of the gods, is the ruler of Gemini and Virgo. Mercury is the messenger in astrology as it is in mythology. It is the planet of day-to-day expression and communication. Now I have found patterns with the planets, where typically they are similar to your SUN sign, but that's not always the case. For example, my SUN sign is Aquarius and oddly enough both my MERCURY and VENUS signs are Aquarius as well. Again, you're going to have to calculate your planets through a calculator (Café Astrology).

ARIES

These communicators make quick decisions—so quick that you might think they don't much like thinking things over. The truth is Aries communicators don't have a lot of patience for mulling. Their decisions are often driven by their need for instant gratification. They are direct and candid, and some may even think their style is crude at times. They can even come across as downright aggressive, but that usually happens when they encounter opposition to their opinions and ideas.

TAURUS

Mercury in Taurus natives are plodders. They may take their time to arrive at a decision, but they get there and are actually quite decisive, even stubborn, with their opinions. Some may mistake the time they take over decisions for laziness, but look a little deeper and you will find that these people do think. They may be slow to start a new project, but they see it through to the end; however, you may need to poke them to get them going. They have much common sense at their disposal.

GEMINI

These folks are generally quick-witted. They can come across as somewhat scattered, and this is mainly due to their eclectic interests. They seem to know a little about everything. Turn to Mercury in Gemini men and women for lots of facts and figures, as well as broad knowledge (perhaps a good partner for trivia night!). Their learning is a little superficial—they generally have too many interests to delve too deeply into any one.

CANCER

These people communicate with feeling, conveying a sensitive, withdrawn, and thoughtful nature to the people they interact with. No matter how free-spirited the rest of their natal charts may be, Mercury in Cancer people can be very subjective and personal, or they opt not to talk at all. They are slow to respond at times, giving others the impression that they are deep thinkers.

LEO

When these people speak, they do it with authority. Some of them come across as know-it-alls, but the more mature ones speak with style. They want others to know about their presence of mind and their know-how. Mercury in Leo men and women are adept at seeing the big picture, sometimes at the cost of ignoring the details. They are generally skilled at the art of persuasion (I bet they make great car salesmen!). While others may try to win people over with logic, guilt, or wit, Mercury in Leo does it with warmth and good will. They are excellent at promoting ideas and getting their message across.

VIRGO

These people are rarely flashy in their communication style, but they do thoroughly appreciate it when others acknowledge their brainpower. These people love to keep track of all the details. They can be a little high-strung when things are not orderly or when things seem out of control, so they put a lot of energy into taking care of day-to-day, practical matters.

LIBRA

These folks come across as very pleasing. Diplomacy comes naturally to these natives. At the very least, they take many pains to be diplomatic. Mercury in Libra people long for equality in the intellectual world.

SCORPIO

These people are on an eternal quest to get to the very heart of any matter. This appears in anything that requires thought and in almost every conversation they have. Totally fearless when it comes to delving into depths that nobody else wants or even thinks to explore, Mercury in Scorpio is adept at learning the source and the core of any problem or issue.

SAGITTARIUS

Freedom of thought is what Mercury in Sagittarius strives for. These people communicate in an optimistic, forward-looking manner. Their ideas are generally very big, but it's probably wise to use tact when you see all the little holes in their arguments. Remember: they mean well. These people have vision.

CAPRICORN

These natives have a strong need to compartmentalize the impressions they get from the world. These people often speak and write in a slow and methodical manner. They appreciate structure and order. Although they are resourceful people, Mercury in Capricorn natives easily get frustrated when too much information is thrown at them at once. They break down ideas into manageable parts before arriving at a decision.

AQUARIUS

Unconventional in self-expression, Mercury in Aquarius natives enjoy breaking the rules. They are not necessarily loud or flamboyant people, but they often have a quiet way of stirring others up. These natives delight in exposing what they deem to be biases in others' ways of thinking. Very quick to contradict others and to offer a different perspective, these natives enjoy intellectual debates. They're very quick and alert, and their powers of observation are particularly strong. They usually "win" debates. In fact, they're very interested in scoring intellectual points, which can be maddening to others at times.

PISCES

These folks are gentle communicators with a soft touch that is pleasing and warm. Some of them come across in an almost poetic way. Not given to bother too much with details, these individuals tend to sponge up the feelings and moods of their environment. The information they extract from their surroundings can be unusual and certainly unique. For some, it is heavily skewed in the direction of emotion and feeling.

Remember:

Mercury is how you communicate, and can be very important in a romantic relationships, since as a relationship expert (my Ph.D.!), communication is the most important tool in any relationship. And next, Venus will be explained and how it can explain your "love style".

VENUS

VENUS is our love style. As someone who studies mate selection, I realize how important it is to understand whether two people's love styles are compatible, especially when they are in a romantic relationship. In a parent or peer relationship, it may be less important, but obviously how we love and want to be loved is always essential in any relationship. Venus is the Goddess of Love. In astrology, VENUS rules our sentiments, what we value, and the pleasure we take in life. Grace, charm, and beauty are all ruled by VENUS. We can then learn about our tastes, pleasures, artistic inclinations, and what makes us happy. Next are some tidbits from the various VENUS love styles and a possible Match.com heading for you singles out there!

ARIES

These people flirt by being upfront, direct, and even daringly. They try to win you over by expressing how enterprising and independent they are. Their style of expressing love can be maddeningly me-centered, but the right person for them will find this approach charming. People get turned on by Venus in Aries aura of innocent charm even when Arians are being childish and impatient.

POSSIBLE MATCH.COM PROFILE: "I have a strong sense of adventure. I will win you over. I'm self-taught and self-sufficient."

TAURUS

These people project themselves as solid and comfortable. In fact, something about their manner promises they will be satisfying lovers and partners. They need a certain measure of predictability and dependability in their relationships.

POSSIBLE MATCH.COM PROFILE: "I am a dependable guy/gal. My ideal date consists of good food, fine wine, and cuddling up with each other at home."

GEMINI

These people will try to win over the object of their affection with witty conversation, displaying just how much they "know" and demonstrating their diverse interests. These lovers are playful—some might even call them a tease. They are hard to pin down, and they resist relationships that promise to become too "comfortable."

POSSIBLE MATCH.COM PROFILE: "I am fun-loving. My ideal date consists of going to a cafe, taking in a movie, and talking about it."

CANCER

Love for Venus in Cancer is best when it is committed and rather predictable. These people are sensitive in love. You may even say their egos are a little underdeveloped when it comes to love, but they have a lot to give in return: namely security, comfort, and care.

POSSIBLE MATCH.COM PROFILE: "I'm just a regular guy/gal. I've built a solid foundation. I'm comfortable and comforting. I care. I stick around. My ideal date consists of eating in and snuggling up to each other."

LEO

When Venus in Leo people are in love, they are proud, even boastful. They love to court and be courted, and they need to feel very special. They are warm, generous, and even grand. Though really quite loyal to their partners (remember that love is THE most important thing for Leos), they thrive on attention from the opposite sex.

POSSIBLE MATCH.COM PROFILE: "I'm warm-hearted and fun. I'm funny and experienced. Let me show you a good time."

VIRGO

Venus in Virgo people are not the flirtatious sort. Instead, their appeal lies in their dedication, their willingness to work on the relationship and make it work in real terms. Their gifts are less showy but perhaps far more generous—gifts of devotion and attention to details about you.

POSSIBLE MATCH.COM PROFILE: "I will care for you and do lots of little things for you. I will help you."

LIBRA

Venus in Libra people will try to impress you with their kindness, evenhandedness, and willingness to make your relationship work. They have a polished manner in love, which sometimes makes them appear insincere or superficial. They are gentle lovers who hate to be offended. They are threatened by bad manners and direct or abrasive expression of feelings. They not only prefer to choose the middle road, they seek the middle ground in their relationships. You can expect to be treated fairly, and you may be turned on by Venus in Libra's willingness to concede and adjust their lives fully to accommodate you.

POSSIBLE MATCH.COM PROFILE: "I'm just a nice guy/gal— some say I'm too nice. I'm romantic and love good conversations. I will please you. All I ask for is fairness."

SCORPIO

Venus in Scorpio people attract others with their intensity and willingness to commit. They have a strong and concentrated manner which suggests their feelings run deep. Their actions in love tend to promise deep commitment and sexual pleasure even if they are not telling you this directly. Their appeal lies in their focus on you and their dedication. Venus in Scorpio seems fearless when it comes to intimacy. Potential lovers get the feeling that Venus in Scorpio will never stray and that they are intensely loyal to the one they love. They possess you and somehow make it seem attractive to be possessed.

POSSIBLE MATCH.COM PROFILE: "I'm emotional and deep. I'll be very loyal, too, forever. I'm looking for commitment. I'll make you happy in bed."

SAGITTARIUS

When Venus in Sagittarius people are in love, they need to feel they can grow and expand their horizons through their relationship. They want to learn new things and experience everything together. These are idealistic lovers who want you to appreciate their beliefs, visions, and ideals. They can be a confusing mix of the lighthearted and serious. They are roamers and seekers and don't commit in their relationships as easily as others.

POSSIBLE MATCH.COM PROFILE: "I am fun and funny. I have joie de vivre and I love to laugh. I am open to experiences."

CAPRICORN

Venus in Capricorn people will try to win your heart by displaying self-control, presence of mind, and responsible behavior. These lovers want you to know they are goal-oriented, witty, savvy, and controlled. Nobody can get the best of them. They want you to see just how competent they are. They like some measure of predictability in their relationships as they are cautious in love.

POSSIBLE MATCH.COM PROFILE: "I have a good job. I invest wisely. I will give you security. Marriage and family are important to me."

AQUARIUS

Venus in Aquarius people try to impress you with their open-minded, future-thinking spirit. They want you to see them as unique, rebellious, and a little provocative. They are attractive when they are acting a little aloof. They want you to acknowledge and appreciate that they don't follow the beaten track in matters of the heart.

POSSIBLE MATCH.COM PROFILE*: "I'm liberal. I'm not possessive. I'm looking for a friend in a lover. I'm unique. Let's talk and have some fun."*

PISCES

Venus in Pisces people project themselves as dreamy, soft-hearted partners. Everything about the way they flirt promises a lovely time. Theirs is an elusive charm—they are sweetly playful, a little moody, and perhaps a little irregular. They appreciate romance and poetry, and they prefer to "feel out" both you and the relationship you share, so don't expect too much planning ahead.

POSSIBLE MATCH.COM PROFILE*: "I will love you for you. I will accept you. Even if the rest of the world thinks you are unlovable, I will see you for what you really are."*

Remember:

Venus represents the way you show and expect love in a relationship. It can be beneficial in knowing if you're clingy, needy, independent, or flirtatious in your romantic relationships, and especially for those people that are dating! But next, what about your conflict style? Do you get angry fast, or do you like to pout and avoid conflict all together? That will be explained by the planet Mars in your birth chart.

MARS

As for MARS, it's our aggressive side and quite telling for some people. Mars, the God of War, is the ruler of Aries. In astrology, MARS is the planet of energy, action, and desire. It is the survival instinct and can be thought of as the "leftover" animal nature of man. MARS rules our animal instincts for aggression, anger, and survival. Our sexual desires come under the rule of MARS. Whereas VENUS rules romantic attraction, MARS is most associated with basic body attraction. This is the planet of action rather than reaction. Here's a quick guide to your MARS style.

ARIES

This is a very impulsive position of Mars. The first instinct for Mars in Aries natives is to take action. Quick flare-ups characterize the Mars in Aries character, but their anger usually doesn't last for too long. In fact, these people generally don't live in the past and are not given to holding grudges or feeling resentful. Generally, their tempers flare quickly, and they deal with anger on issues right away—with this kind of character, there is little room for festering.

TAURUS

Slow and steady wins the race could easily be a motto for Mars in Taurus. These goal-oriented people are not known for their speed, but their staying power is tremendous. Generally calm and easygoing people, Mars in Taurus natives can have powerful tempers when they're overly provoked. They generally don't fly off the handle as quickly as others.

GEMINI

Easily bored, Mars in Gemini natives need a fresh change of pace frequently just to keep energy levels up. It's a somewhat odd thing really. When there's nothing much to do, these natives are exhausted. But if there's plenty of interesting things on their agenda, Mars in Gemini natives can be powerhouses! More than most people, these individuals have a physical reaction to boredom.

CANCER

This position inclines toward passive-aggressiveness. These people seem to resist change and to shy away from direct confrontations. They need to feel secure before they act. As a result, they can appear rather slow at times. Their motto is "The best offense is a good defense." They may appear weak to some, but they can be very strong. Their strength lies in their tenacity.

LEO

This position of Mars gives a drive for significance. Mars in Leo individuals possess a strong need to create in some way—and they are determined that their lives have not only meaning but also significant meaning! Passions run high and so does desire. There is a strong will that gives these natives much staying power. Though Mars in Leo people will enjoy the pleasures of risk-taking, they generally have a strong sense of reason at the end of the day.

VIRGO

These productive and busy people are goal-oriented practical people. Although they can be a little scattered at times, simply because they are doing so many things at any given time, Mars in Virgo natives get things done—quite well! They have a knack for handling a wide variety of tasks at once and a tendency to take on perhaps too much at the same time. Most Mars in Virgo natives are not particularly aggressive by nature. Although they can be a little hard-nosed and critical at times, they rarely resort to pushing others around. Still, an annoyed Mars in Virgo native can be difficult to be around! Arouse their anger and they turn into complaining, over-critical nags.

LIBRA

Mars in Libra natives often reflect about things before they act. Decisiveness is not their strong point, but they do eventually get things done. Many people with this position procrastinate—generally because they feel the need to weigh all of the alternatives before taking action.

SCORPIO

Mars in Scorpio natives love to challenge themselves to do the impossible. They throw themselves into what they decide to do with concentrated energy and awesome willpower. These people make formidable opponents although often quietly so. They keep their cool and their equilibrium on the surface. Below the surface may be another story, and they are unlikely to easily let you in. Mars in Scorpio has the potential to exploit others. These people see through others and rely heavily on their gut feelings.

SAGITTARIUS

When Mars in Sagittarius people get angry, they feel like running. They have to do something—not about it—but something else altogether. They don't have a lot of patience to wait things out. This is where the restless and adventurous nature of Sagittarius comes in. People with this position of Mars should seriously consider physical activity as the best means of anger management if they don't already (naturally) do so.

CAPRICORN

Natives with this position have a subdued and controlled style of approaching life. Most don't come across as particularly enthusiastic; rather, theirs is a low-key but determined energy. Mars in Capricorn natives like to be on top of things. They are generally goal-oriented and focused people who are not afraid of hard work. Most are achievers by nature, and many possess well-defined ambitions—well-defined to themselves more than anything. They're not particularly flashy people, but their drive to succeed and to make their lives secure is strong even if it's not right out there for the world to see.

AQUARIUS

It can be a little difficult to understand exactly what makes a Mars in Aquarius native tick. And that's absolutely fine with them—they enjoy surprising people. The tried-and-true methods of getting things done are far too boring for those born with Mars in this unique and original sign. Mars in Aquarius natives often have a rather original view of the world as well. These natives are generally quite proud of their independence. They are not easily pushed around with Mars in this fixed sign.

PISCES

Mild-tempered and gentle, these guys and gals move through life in a manner that can hardly be considered direct. Mars is the planet of action and assertion, and Pisces is a passive sign that rarely asserts itself in a direct fashion. So the placement of Mars in Pisces is an unusual combination. Sometimes prone to feelings of guilt about their anger and difficulties with asserting themselves, Mars in Pisces individuals seem to go with the flow. This is certainly not a very active position for Mars, and natives will often let life happen instead of trying to control their life direction. This is a charming position as individuals with Mars in Pisces don't appear like they are capable of harming a fly. However, those that don't find creative expression for this energy can stir up a storm through indirect aggression.

Remember:

Mars represents your conflict style, and thus, is an extremely important ingredient in your romantic relationships. Conflict will happen in every romantic partnership, but how you fight is the key. Next, we'll discuss people who fall in between two signs, known as Cuspers, and why they are so unique.

1/2 TSP CUSPS

If you're not familiar with the meaning of Cusps, then you're not alone. It's not often discussed on many astrology websites or in books. Cusps refers to falling in between two signs, typically around the 18th–22nd of each month, so if your birthday is one of those numbers, then most likely you are a Cusper. These individuals are quite unique and have the potential to have multiple personalities— but in a good way. They may have strengths and weaknesses from two distinct zodiac signs which may explain why they are a little more unique than someone with their same zodiac sign. I've read that Cuspers are more attracted to other fellow Cuspers, so perhaps they are drawn to each other in some unique way, but decide for yourself. Here's a great website that discusses the Cusps: http://www.dailyhoroscope.com/ free-astrology/born-on-the-cusp and a quick breakdown of each one follows.

ARIES/TAURUS CUSP

Those born on the Cusp of Power between about April 16 to April 24 are indeed a force to be reckoned with. Authoritative and bold, Aries-Taurus cuspers are natural born leaders. They'll take charge at work or at home, and the two signs energies mix well for success– impulsive Aries lends energy and pushes forward toward goals while practical Taurus takes care of all the details. One area to watch is that of being too forceful and barreling right over the opinions and desires of others.

TAURUS/GEMINI CUSP

Those born between about May 16 to May 24 are one of the most youthful, go-getting cuspers of all! Those born on this cusp have the bonus of being both physically strong and mentally agile, which makes them stable and driven, as well as clever and communicative. Such traits give these cuspers the ability to adapt to too many different situations and people and to want to do it all—and to do it a lot.

GEMINI/CANCER CUSP

Those born between about June 19 and June 24 are on a magical cusp, and their lives will be an inspiration to others. Caring and devoted, those born on this cusp infuse the world around them with lighthearted kindness and are able to find inspiration in the ordinary—then share what they've learned with others. The effect can be truly inspiring. These cuspers can be quite talkative, yet emotional. Thus they may enjoy gossip!

CANCER/LEO CUSP

Those born between about July 19 to July 26 were born of a conflicting mix of water and fire and can be shy and sensitive one moment and gregarious drama queens the next. The danger here is that they might be either so sensitive or so insensitive that they'll come across as self-absorbed either way.

LEO/VIRGO CUSP

Those born between about August 18 to August 26 were born on the Cusp of Exposure—which isn't nearly as naughty as it sounds. In fact, these cuspers are more likely to be found working hard, arguing their positions on issues or studying new intellectual pursuits than they are of playing around, but that doesn't mean they aren't any fun. There's a bit of conflicting energy to these souls that arises from Leo's need for drama and attention and Virgo's more antisocial tendencies; therefore, it's not uncommon for them to go to one extreme or the other: loud and direct or silent and secretive.

VIRGO/LIBRA CUSP

Those born between about September 19 and September 24, The Cusp of Beauty, are ruled by both Mercury and Venus—respectively, the planet of communication and the planet of love. Sounds like a pretty delightful combination, right? It is, indeed. Beauty cuspers are balanced—with sensitivities to both their internal and external worlds. They are deep thinkers who often are physically attractive, too! They are drawn to aesthetically pleasing people, objects, art and nature and are quick to keep up with the latest trends.

LIBRA/SCORPIO CUSP

Those born between about October 19 and October 27 will likely inherit some dynamic qualities from Libra and Scorpio for they are born on the Cusp of Drama and Criticism. The end result is a powerful combination of intellect, drive, flamboyance and sexuality that will wow the masses—but may prove too much for some to handle.

SCORPIO/SAGITTARIUS CUSP

Those born on the Cusp of Revolution between about November 19 to 26 are full of strength and rebellious energy. Individuals born on this cusp possess the bold, aggressive qualities of Scorpio along with the active and adaptable traits of Sagittarius. They are likely to be accomplished because they have that intense Scorpio passion combined with the typical Sagittarius way of charging right into action. Sometimes they are so action-oriented that they can be characterized as rebellious—and maybe even accused of running wild!

SAGITTARIUS/CAPRICORN CUSP

Those born between about December 16 and December 26, the Cusp of Prophecy, are an ideal blend of optimist and pragmatist. These cuspers have both the vision to create successful ideas and the determination and drive to make them a reality. Having a birthday on the cusp of these two Sun signs alone points to unparalleled success.

CAPRICORN/AQUARIUS CUSP

Those born between about January 14 and January 26, the Cusp of Mystery and Imagination, will never experience a dull moment. Whether outwardly flamboyant or shy and quiet, these cuspers always have much excitement going on internally. They have vivid dreams and rich fantasies that need to be expressed creatively if they're to be happy. Prone to leading unusual lives, Capriquarians often will struggle to balance the two very different sides of their personalities. They are reserved yet social, security-craving but independent, and traditional yet offbeat. They love to talk and entertain, and they especially enjoy intellectually stimulating conversations about any manner of strange topics. This is why no matter how hard they work or how dedicated they are to achieving their goals, things are never dull. While hard-work and high standards bring these cuspers much success in most career endeavors, they can have more difficulty maintaining personal relationships. This is perhaps due to a need for independence and a tendency to seem aloof and critical—sometimes even selfish. However, if they can put forth the loyal, funny and friendly sides of themselves, they'll make friends easily.

AQUARIUS/PISCES CUSP

Those born between about February 16 to 26 on the Cusp of Sensitivity are rooted in compassion and imaginative thinking. Spiritual, artistic, peace-loving and friendly, these cuspers are highly original people. This is the cusp most likely to be labeled "offbeat" or "eccentric," and its citizens are stimulated by visionary ideas and new experiences. They are highly intellectual; however, they are not so good with practical details and follow-through. These cuspers may be social or shy, or they may be a peculiar mix of both. This is because spending time with others is a great stress relief, but at the same time they are so sensitive they often choose to hide out alone and escape into their imaginations instead.

PISCES/ARIES CUSP

Individuals born between about March 16 to March 24 are an intriguing mix of fiery impulsiveness and imaginative daydreaming, which is actually pretty excellent because it means they're both doers and dreamers. A bit impatient and very direct, Pisarians can sometimes rub others the wrong way by refusing to compromise. Why compromise when you are always right, they wonder? At the same time this does make them great leaders.

Remember:

Cuspers are generally those who fall in between two zodiacs, or in the middle of every month essentially. They encompass both signs, which may explain why they are so unique and different from others with the same sign.

Again, you need to gather all the basic ingredients to fully understand someone: birth date, birth time, and birth location. The birth chart will help you understand yourself and your relationships by understanding the different ingredients, such as the Sun, Moon, Ascendant, planets, and whether any of you fall on a cusp.

Chapter 3
Sun Compatibilities

"There shall be signs in the sun, the moon, and the stars." - Luke 21:25

Ok so we've now read about the important ingredients that comprise individuals, based on their zodiac birth charts, but now we get to the good stuff—the compatibilities between people! Each person (or sign) obviously has different strengths and weaknesses. Some people are open-minded and optimistic, and some people are very set in their ways and have a pessimistic outlook. Your sign is determined by the date, month, and year in which you were born and indicates how you might interact with people born under the various signs. Some people are very compatible as friends or business partners, and some are compatible as romantic partners.

Compatibility in a long term relationship involves so much more than just physical attraction. If your partner has a hard time showing emotions, is it better for your relationship if you are open with your emotions? Is it true that "birds of a feather flock together or opposites attract"? So many things factor into a blissfully happy and compatible relationship. This next section focuses on different recipe combinations of zodiac SUN signs, but again, this is only one ingredient into really understanding the entire recipe of yourself and your relationships. You will need to look at all the other compatibilities between the MOON signs, the PLANETS, etc.

Next, let's examine the SUN sign recipe relationship combinations. (Note: I did not repeat any, and the Cuspers are not included here.)

ARIES

ARIES-TAURUS

While it is fairly typical for an ARIES periodically to become gripped with an idea and feel that the time to act on this idea is now, a TAURUS prefers to fully digest the whole idea and respond to situations with a more practical and cautious attitude. If ARIES stumbles or fails, then TAURUS may react with an "I told you so" attitude. This can be infuriating to ARIES and very detrimental to the relationship. Learning to appreciate one another's very different approach to life will be very beneficial for both of them. For example, TAURUS can help supply the reliability and consistent dedication needed to help bring ARIES's ideas and impulses to a fruitful completion. Both of them should try to adapt to each other's style in daily events, too. The TAURUS may initially resist a sudden impulse of ARIES to go somewhere when joining in the fun would be much more satisfying for both of them. They have very different rhythms. ARIES is quicker but less persistent and steady than TAURUS.

ARIES-GEMINI

Both enjoy and need to be active and on the go and are more interested in the present than the past. Once something has outlived its usefulness, they are both ready to part with it and go on to something new. Both have a low tolerance for boredom! They also share a weakness in common: the inability to stick with things (projects and relationships) when they become dull or problematic. Neither want a very clingy, dependent type of partner; with one another they have a certain amount of independence that both enjoy. Sometimes GEMINI wants to discuss an idea while ARIES becomes impatient with the conversation, feeling that GEMINI is beating around the bush and not really getting to the heart of the matter. Then ARIES becomes abrupt, impatient, and tactless at such times. GEMINI must realize that ARIES simply does not have a taste for conversation at such times and must not rely too much on ARIES for daily conversation. Handled positively, GEMINI can provide lots of different perspectives on ARIES's impulsive ideas.

ARIES-CANCER

ARIES often feels smothered by demands of family and even friends. CANCER, on the other hand, is very devoted to family needs and the inner, emotional needs of others. Without realizing it, ARIES may selfishly accept CANCER's nurturing and giving while contributing relatively little to the relationship on an emotional level. ARIES's need for autonomy and independence often conflicts with CANCER's needs for closeness, intimacy, and mutual dependency. ARIES seems selfish, impersonal, and indifferent to CANCER at times, and CANCER may feel too needy and emotionally sensitive to ARIES. ARIES can learn compassion from CANCER, and CANCER can learn to be more independent, but it's likely to be a rough road at times with much adjustment needed on both sides.

ARIES-LEO (best compatibility)

Both are independent, self-motivated individuals, very much concerned with their own creative work and interests and prefer not to feel like they are "owned" in a relationship. ARIES, however, often acts in a manner that is socially inappropriate while LEO is more aware of appearances and is more concerned with the response of others. ARIES is somewhat indifferent to other people's opinions while LEO craves approval and affirmation from others. Both are immensely proud and neither wants to take the back seat in this relationship. There is a great deal of harmony between them, but being two spirited and somewhat volatile people, when they clash, their fights are likely to be dramatic and boisterous.

ARIES-VIRGO

Honesty and a desire for the unadorned truth are virtues both possess and value although VIRGO takes ARIES's honest criticism better than ARIES takes VIRGO's. Some very basic differences in their makeup can make them uncomfortable with each other at times: ARIES tends to throw caution to the wind while VIRGO worries a great deal if all details are not taken care of first. ARIES acts now on impulse and intuition while VIRGO wants to think carefully and study the fine print first. VIRGO is the more self-analytical of the two, and ARIES is likely to be impatient with this at times. VIRGO also tends to be more giving and may get into the role of assistant or "servant" to ARIES. Both need to make a lot of adjustments in order to accommodate their differences. However, they can certainly learn from each other, and the differences in personalities can be very attractive to both of them.

ARIES-LIBRA

There is a basic difference in personalities in this relationship. LIBRA likes to look at both sides of an issue and consider any situation from every angle. LIBRA also likes to discuss ideas with others and get their opinion, but sometimes still has difficulty coming to a definitive decision. ARIES is prone to be just the opposite—taking a strong, more one-sided view of a situation and frequently is uninterested in hearing others' points of view. In order for this relationship to work, they will have to reconcile this basic difference in their personalities. Over time, LIBRA may feel that ARIES is a selfish egotist, and ARIES may feel that LIBRA is a weak-willed wimp. Obviously, both will need to have greater appreciation and respect for each other than this! LIBRA makes many more compromises and accommodations for the relationship than ARIES does.

ARIES-SCORPIO

Both are both willful and passionate people with a strong desire to live intensely and directly and love this about each other. There is a lot of fire in their relationship, so they are likely to fight ferociously sometimes. ARIES, however, can release anger and emotions and then forget about it while SCORPIO nurses grudges and resentments and may hold onto the wounds that ARIES unthinkingly inflicts. Also, SCORPIO needs to feel intensely bonded emotionally, and ARIES may not have the same overwhelming need for closeness.

ARIES-SAGITTARIUS (excellent)

Enthusiasm, a sense of adventure, and high spirited play infuse this relationship. Both feel they can be themselves fully with one another: they don't have to tone down any of their exuberance and energy, the way they might with someone else. In fact, they inspire and vitalize one another's strength. ARIES sometimes clashes or competes with other strong individuals, but SAGITTARIUS is tolerant, not threatened, and doesn't take the bait. Also, both need personal freedom and space, and even if they spend all of their time together, they are unlikely to feel smothered in this relationship. A happy twosome!

ARIES-CAPRICORN

Both of these are active, motivated individuals, but ARIES's focus is more on being self-reliant, independent and personally creative while CAPRICORN likes to follow a well-planned, stable path to success. ARIES feels very constrained and inhibited by social norms, schedules and employers while CAPRICORN works well where there is a clear hierarchy and social order, such as in a large business, college curriculum, or military pecking order. ARIES's impulsiveness and indifference to social customs clashes with CAPRICORN's conservatism sometimes. However, ARIES can also give CAPRICORN sober encouragement, hope, and enthusiasm, and CAPRICORN can help ARIES organize and direct abundant energy.

ARIES-AQUARIUS

Both are independent, active individuals who appreciate progressive, dynamic approaches to any situation or problem, and the relationship has a lively, spirited quality. Both can be iconoclasts as well, taking pride in freedom from many traditional values and beliefs. ARIES is more concerned with personal creativity and in some ways is less integrated into social groups and the community than AQUARIUS. They appreciate and respect one another's uniqueness and individuality.

ARIES-PISCES

ARIES is more decisive and direct but also somewhat more naive and simple (psychologically speaking) than PISCES is. They balance one another nicely. ARIES depends on PISCES's sensitivity and gentleness to soothe, heal, and provide a sanctuary from the world of competing and achieving. PISCES, on the other hand, admires and probably needs ARIES's forthrightness, honesty, and willingness to act boldly. PISCES is more of a giver and can be very self-denying while ARIES is self-absorbed and can unintentionally take advantage of PISCES's generosity. ARIES also lacks tact and subtlety sometimes and inadvertently wounds PISCES's tender feelings.

ARIES-ARIES

Both are independent individuals who don't like feeling "owned" by anyone. Neither can tolerate being dominated or bossed by anyone else, so they probably will make their own decisions and direct their own lives in this relationship. They respect one another's autonomy, and a relationship that is based on constant togetherness and dependency wouldn't suit either of them. Sometimes, however, there is too much emphasis on individualism rather than on being close and nurturing the relationship. Both have proud egos and are sensitive to criticism. Almost inevitably they will compete with each other. In small doses this can be invigorating, but it can easily become nasty, and one is likely to get hurt. If you've ever seen two rams locking horns, you know what I mean! They either respect one another immensely or detest one another—rarely anything in between.

TAURUS

TAURUS-GEMINI

TAURUS is stable, grounded, and steady—qualities that GEMINI lacks and feels both drawn to and impatient with sometimes. TAURUS is intrigued by and respects GEMINI's wit, mental agility and intelligence but is sometimes annoyed with GEMINI's inability to make a commitment or to follow through on intentions. GEMINI likes to talk and can jump rapidly from one topic to the next in rapid succession. TAURUS, on the other hand, likes to methodically digest one topic at a time and quickly gets "mental indigestion" from GEMINI's fast-paced conversation. When faced with an important decision, for example, TAURUS would benefit by taking a quiet walk in the woods or along the beach while GEMINI needs to talk with someone. Both must learn to respect each other's different styles or will certainly get in each other's way.

TAURUS-CANCER (excellent combo)

Both are very domestic and appreciate the simple joys of life. Others find the two of them to be very warm, friendly, and caring, and a soft and considerate attitude is greatly appreciated by friends. If they have children, then they will be very dedicated and involved parents. The two of them would enjoy living in a quiet, fairly secluded place away from hustle and bustle. CANCER is very emotional, very attached to family and familiar surroundings and easily upset by any form of cruelty; TAURUS's practical, grounded approach to life and gentle manner is very much appreciated by CANCER.

TAURUS-LEO

Both are strong-willed and stubborn, and once they dedicate themselves to a person or a project, they will stay with it in good times and bad. Longevity, stability, and loyalty characterize this relationship. Both can be infuriatingly obstinate and inflexible at times, and their personal styles and tastes often conflict. For instance, LEO is a more social creature, who wants to go out more often and is more daring and colorful than TAURUS. LEO will spend or gamble more freely than TAURUS. Even though they thoroughly disagree sometimes, their commitment is always strong and rarely questioned. They KNOW they can depend on one another. Both are so resistant to change that even if they hated each other, it would be hard for them to disengage themselves and move on! Also, they need to guard against becoming so self-satisfied and comfortable in their relationship that they take one another for granted.

TAURUS-VIRGO (excellent)

These two have a very harmonious and helpful relationship. They are both very practical people and work effectively as partners in work or in marriage. They can build a rich and rewarding life together, for they are able to devote themselves completely to one another (and their children if they have any). TAURUS is steadier emotionally than VIRGO, and VIRGO appreciates TAURUS's consistent nurturing, healing, and soothing qualities. They share a great interest in food; VIRGO is especially concerned with nutrition and is somewhat fastidious while TAURUS just thoroughly enjoys it! This is likely to be a long-lasting relationship.

TAURUS-LIBRA

Both are lovers of peace and harmony and avoid conflict and tension as much as possible. There is a cordial, soft quality to their relationship that makes it very pleasant, and these qualities draw many friends and acquaintances to them as well. Beneath the smooth facade, however, they do have their differences! Very often LIBRA is more socially oriented and communicative while TAURUS is too busy with interests, hobbies, or work and is not willing to join LIBRA in conversation, social activity, or entertainment. TAURUS needs to be more flexible at times. Aesthetics are also very important to both of them, but they probably disagree on matters of style from time to time.

TAURUS-SCORPIO

There is a strong magnetic attraction between them. Even if they have little in common intellectually or spiritually, their physical relationship is likely to be very intense, binding them together. Even if they do not have common interests and resonate on an intellectual level, they will be unable to stay away from each other! They are both very possessive, and SCORPIO especially is prone to jealousy. There are significant differences in their emotional makeup, however: TAURUS is steadier, simpler, less complex, and less needy than SCORPIO, who demands more in terms of emotional involvement and depth of intimacy than TAURUS. Both are extremely stubborn, strong-willed individuals who need to learn to bend and compromise more graciously in order to harmonize with one another. Neither are especially articulate or communicative about the things that matter most to them, and misunderstandings can result.

TAURUS-SAGITTARIUS

While SAGITTARIUS thrives on variety, travel, socializing, and exploring, TAURUS is often content to plug away at the same thing day after day until it nearly drives SAGITTARIUS crazy! In some ways, they are the "odd couple" with opposite traits. Although it is nice to think that opposite natures can complement each other, the truth is that these two may also need to do many things separately in order to be happy with each other, or SAGITTARIUS is likely to become bored by TAURUS's routine, and TAURUS is likely to feel very distracted and unsettled from SAGITTARIUS's wide-ranging interests. If they can appreciate and understand each other, they will bring balance to their lives.

TAURUS-CAPRICORN (excellent)

Both are very practical people with good common sense. Their grounded and realistic approach to issues makes them very compatible philosophically and intellectually. Over time they may become too complacent and conservative and focus too much on mundane affairs or narrowly focused mental interests. They must take time for sheer fun and enjoyment and not become too serious. They feel they can rely on one another. They can also accomplish a lot together: CAPRICORN is a good organizer and strategist, and

TAURUS will follow through with any joint plan. They make a good team.

TAURUS-AQUARIUS

While TAURUS often takes a practical, down-to-earth, simple approach to life, AQUARIUS is more inclined to take a modern, progressive or unconventional approach. These two often differ on political and social issues as well as have different tastes in art, music, and literature. AQUARIUS is more aware of modern trends and stays more in tune with changing styles and current events while TAURUS stubbornly holds onto the classics. TAURUS's interests are more focused, less wide-ranging, and change little over time. This difference in their approaches to life is not likely to create serious problems, but it does tend to be annoying at times. Both are stubborn (TAURUS is particularly stubborn!), and this can aggravate the problem since they may be unwilling to fully accept and appreciate each other fully. Thus they may also be unwilling to adapt to their differences.

TAURUS-PISCES

Both are basically tolerant, easy-going, "soft" and peace-loving people, and this goes a long way toward maintaining harmony in their relationship. PISCES really appreciates TAURUS's steadiness and dependability while TAURUS responds to PISCES's gentleness, kindness, and sympathy. However, there are also very basic differences between them: TAURUS seeks clear and simple answers, approaches life in a pragmatic, down-to-earth manner, has clear preferences and dislikes, and has very predictable tastes. In addition, TAURUS seeks tangible and clear results from any effort. PISCES, on the other hand, is more eclectic in approach, sensitive to a wider spectrum of ideas and feelings, and is less rational, more emotional, intuitive, and more willing to accept ambiguities and complexities than TAURUS.

TAURUS-TAURUS

Both are very reliable, practical, dedicated individuals. They love natural surroundings and natural beauty and would do well to live in a quiet area rich in natural beauty. Both have a lazy, sensual side and reinforce this in one another. They really enjoy life and its pleasures together. Also, they are both very stubborn and inflexible individuals. Though both prefer domestic harmony, they both cling tenaciously to an opinion and position if they think they are right. Over time, their combined reliability, stability, and practicality is likely to make them very comfortable and materially successful, but their interactions can easily become routine, lacking enthusiasm and zest.

GEMINI

GEMINI-CANCER

CANCER is usually the one who takes care of family affairs—writing letters to family members, visiting family members, providing the emotional support and care needed by children (and adults!), and, in general, is more attentive to people's feelings and emotional needs. CANCER is also more attached to the past, fond memories, places, and friends than GEMINI. Sometimes GEMINI is indifferent to the concerns of CANCER and often simply cannot become as emotionally involved about an issue or situation as CANCER. Even caring, sensitive GEMINIs express their concerns differently and less personally than CANCERs. GEMINI often wants to approach problems intellectually by discussing them whereas CANCER seeks a change in attitude and feels that talking often evades the underlying problems. Many of the misunderstandings between these individuals arise because GEMINI is more emotionally detached and rational while CANCER is more subjective, emotionally involved, and unable to be as articulate and "reasonable" as GEMINI. Paradoxically, they are attracted to one another for the same reason! GEMINI's mental agility and wit appeals to CANCER while CANCER's sensitivity and depth of feeling is attractive to GEMINIs. Both have much to learn from one another.

GEMINI-LEO

Both have a very childlike, playful, fun-loving side that is brought out when you are together. Both love drama and color, and find one another to be delightful and interesting. GEMINI is more intellectual than LEO, however, and needs a variety of people, activities, and interests in order to be happy. LEO wants to be the most important person in GEMINI's life and may not appreciate all of GEMINI's other interests and friendships. LEO makes commitments and keeps them better than GEMINI does because LEO is less restless. Once having found something good, LEO sticks with it and doesn't completely understand GEMINI's desire for novelty. Also, LEO is very proud and has a sensitive ego while GEMINI can be a merciless teaser and doesn't always take LEO seriously. For the most part, however, they are great friends and can be very compatible lovers.

GEMINI-VIRGO

These two are both intellectual creatures, more rational than emotional, and have a good mental rapport. Both love to talk, and appreciate one another's wit. VIRGO, however, has a more practical, down-to-earth turn of mind while GEMINI just enjoys playing with ideas without needing a purpose or practical application for them. GEMINI is also more of a risk-taker and will gladly do something once "just for the experience" while VIRGO is more careful, cautious, and discriminating. For the most part, however, they understand each other well and can be quite compatible.

GEMINI-LIBRA (excellent)

Both have an excellent mental rapport and enjoy one another's intelligence, wit, and style. Both are very social creatures who thrive on interaction with people, cultural activities and conversation. This match is likely to be a very egalitarian one, for both want a partner who is an equal and a friend above all else. LIBRA is very considerate, has a strong desire to please GEMINI (or any partner), will compromise readily and always sees numerous possibilities or desirable alternatives. Both these individuals have trouble being decisive or making up their minds sometimes.

GEMINI-SCORPIO

These two are very different! SCORPIO becomes intensely involved emotionally to particular people and places, bonds deeply and becomes very attached to close people and especially to a lover. By contrast, GEMINI, takes life in a lighter vein and usually does not become as emotionally involved and attached to things as SCORPIO.

SCORPIO may feel that GEMINI is superficial, evasive, childish, and not serious enough while GEMINI may feel that SCORPIO is too heavy, intense, demanding, and insatiable. SCORPIO thrives on intensive, direct experiences and is best suited to a lifestyle that involves direct, non-vicarious, non-intellectual activities of forceful, instinctive, or natural kind, preferably using one's hands (examples: surgery, deep sea diving, most competitive athletic sports, sex, pottery, etc.) while GEMINI's approach is more cerebral, less focused and intensive, and more varied. The disparity between these two approaches to life is great, and they need to strive to make their differences complement each other rather than interfere with each other. The truth is they are probably attracted to the very same qualities that make them so different.

GEMINI-SAGITTARIUS ("heaven or hell," i.e., Brad Pitt and Angelina Jolie)

Both are curious individuals, rather restless and on-the-go. They can expect their lives together to be very active and filled with lots of changes: probably frequent moves, adjustments, surprises, and new challenges. These changes will bring lots of ups and downs, but overall both will be greatly enriched by these diverse activities and interests. SAGITTARIUS is more philosophical and has grander plans than GEMINI, who takes each step as it comes and finds more pleasure in the little things in life. SAGITTARIUS enjoys being on a crusade or mission for some philosophical reason or for personal gain while GEMINI finds SAGITTARIUS's dreams and schemes entertaining and interesting. They often see things from a different perspective but usually can benefit from each other's viewpoints because they are adaptable and flexible enough to listen to each other and benefit from each other. Personal freedom is important to both of them, and they are likely to find it in this relationship. Even if they are always together, they do not cling to or smother one another. On the whole they are very compatible.

GEMINI-CAPRICORN

The two of them are very different! CAPRICORN approaches life in a much more methodical, planned, patient manner than GEMINI. CAPRICORN uses a clear strategy and is willing to work hard for many long years to gradually achieve the intended goal. CAPRICORN is capable of great reliability and dedication and will, for example, be willing to work through years of school until the desired degree is achieved or work through a business or government hierarchy until a top position is achieved. GEMINI may also be successful, but the route is very different. GEMINI succeeds through curiosity, flexibility, adaptability, and communication skills. Unlike CAPRICORN, GEMINI is not inclined to persevere through the dry periods but rather moves on to more interesting material once a point of stagnation is reached. Both approaches can work, but they are different, and they may reach points in their lives where they cannot come to an agreement on the proper path to take. CAPRICORN often seems like the adult in the relationship and can feel too conservative or serious to GEMINI. GEMINI is more like the child (or adolescent), being more flexible and playful but also less reliable and consistent.

GEMINI-AQUARIUS (excellent)

Although they are different people, they might find that their basic goals and outlook in life are compatible. They have an excellent intellectual rapport. They spark each other's wit and love to toss ideas back and forth. Intellectual companionship is important to both of them, and in this relationship they have found a partner whose conversation and company they enjoy. They have the potential to be very good friends, not just lovers. Shared viewpoints, common interests, and social activities are key elements in their relationship. Any relationship will have its challenges, but the two of them share a pleasing overall rapport that can help smooth over other differences.

GEMINI-PISCES

Both are very open-minded, adaptable and flexible individuals, who are receptive to many different points of view and ideas. They are both also quite changeable and fluid and sometimes inconsistent. If looking for a steadying hand or a rock of Gibraltar, look elsewhere. GEMINI approaches situations or problems in a more cerebral, rational manner while PISCES relies more on intuition and feelings. GEMINI may sometimes try to force PISCES to directly discuss an issue, but those attempts will be futile. PISCES may not be able to articulate ideas in as convincing a way as GEMINI, but PISCES tends to draw upon a level of wisdom and sensitivity that is very deep though difficult to formulate clearly in words. GEMINI is more factual, like a reporter, and PISCES is more of a poet. Both must remember that there is truth in both ways of understanding the world. GEMINI finds PISCES ineffable and enigmatic at times. PISCES find GEMINI's nervous energy and hectic pace rather unnerving.

GEMINI-GEMINI

Both are curious, witty, and talkative people. Like children, they love to explore, enjoy variety, become easily bored, and don't take life as seriously as most other people. They enjoy the companionship and intellectual playfulness of one another. They both love to talk. Variety and change are the bread and butter of their lives, and although they may occasionally wish that life was more settled and less hectic, they know that such an existence would be much too dull for them! They have certain potential weaknesses in common, which come to the forefront when they are together: they are too ready to give up on a project or a relationship when it becomes difficult or demanding. They also tend to live in their heads and avoid paying attention to their feelings. Together they may get caught up in word games, intellectual sparring, and light banter. They use humor to gloss over serious topics and deep emotional issues.

CANCER

CANCER-LEO

Both take life very personally, probably more personally than they realize. Their feelings and pride are easily wounded by criticism or lack of appreciation from the people they care about. There can be an unusually warm loving bond between them even though their temperaments are quite different. LEO is very proud and wants recognition, appreciation, respect, and love from a partner. CANCER wants to be needed and desires sympathy, tenderness, and emotional support from a partner. LEO has difficulty accepting and expressing needs, sadness, or weakness, and is uncomfortable when CANCER expresses doubts, insecurities, weaknesses, or moodiness. LEO is the more dominant of the two and is likely to take the lead in their relationship, which is fine with CANCER, who has no need to be on top.

CANCER-VIRGO

Both are inclined to mood changes that at times can irritate one another. For example, CANCER experiences periods of melancholy, tenderness, concern, worry, nostalgia and sentimentality, which VIRGO may not understand or sympathize with. VIRGO can suddenly become irritated and irascible over minor annoyances, and at such times is capable of intense sarcasm and criticism, which can be extremely disconcerting to CANCER's tender, sensitive feelings. VIRGO must be prudent, and CANCER must strive to be forgiving when things go a little awry. However, both are capable of enormous devotion to one another and to their children if they have them. Taking care of one another comes naturally to them.

CANCER-LIBRA

There are some similarities between them and also some significant differences in their temperaments and needs. Both are thoughtful, considerate, and sensitive to and aware of other people's needs. Having good personal relationships is very important to both of them, and they make harmony and peace in their personal lives a very high priority. Both avoid conflict and confrontation if at all possible. The differences are thus: LIBRA is more objective, rational, and fair compared to CANCER, who is subjective, emotional, and biased by personal sympathies and loyalties. Though seemingly sympathetic, LIBRA can be surprisingly cool and intellectual when problems arise the relationship. CANCER responds very personally and emotionally. LIBRA needs more communication and conversation than CANCER does. Also, LIBRA wants to relate as an equal and a peer while CANCER wants to mother or be mothered by a partner. So CANCER is more comfortable with becoming emotionally or financially dependent on a partner or having the partner dependent in that way while LIBRA wants a more egalitarian relationship. These differences can cause misunderstandings between them, but rarely are they a source of major conflict.

CANCER-SCORPIO (most like "soul mates;" i.e., Tom Hanks and Rita Wilson)

It is so very easy for these two to attach themselves to each other! Because each of them possesses a powerful feeling and a tendency to bond intensely with important people in their lives, they sense in each other a basic similarity in temperaments and goals. There are differences, of course, in their natures, but this overall similarity can strengthen the bond between them. CANCER often feels more compassion and sympathy for others while SCORPIO may view CANCER's feelings as sentimentality. When wounded, SCORPIO sometimes tends towards being resentful. CANCER, on the other hand, is more apt to sulk or withdraw when hurt and usually lets the other person know about it (generally in a nonverbal manner!). SCORPIO, by contrast, hides hurt more readily. These two may also have different attitudes towards sexuality versus love. For example, CANCER may feel that SCORPIO is sometimes more driven by instinct and lust than by love, and this may become an issue in their relationship. Overall though, the intense bonding and emotionality of their relationship fosters a deep, lasting attachment between them. Intimacy is likely to come more easily to them as a couple than it does for others, and loyalty is important to both of them.

CANCER-SAGITTARIUS

Their natures are so different that they are bound to clash at times. Very often when SAGITTARIUS feels the urge to travel, explore, expand, and follow a new star, CANCER feels just the opposite: the urge to be close to family, to establish roots, to have children and provide for them, and to be near close friends. SAGITTARIUS's desire for freedom and exploration is often at odds with CANCER's need for security. SAGITTARIUS tends to also be philosophical and detached about personal matters while CANCER takes a much more personal, subjective, compassionate, and emotional approach to life. Although in theory their differences can complement each other, and sometimes they do, there are times when they will have to be very creative and imaginative to find ways to meet both of their needs.

CANCER-CAPRICORN

In many ways these two are opposites. CANCER needs a lot of domestic and family activities. Nurturing others and personal involvement with others is a necessary part of life for CANCER. Family and close friends are extremely important for CANCER while CAPRICORN often becomes emotionally detached from personal affairs and may fail to fully appreciate CANCER's more personal, emotional responses to situations. CAPRICORN may seem dry and perhaps overly ambitious to CANCER. Their differences can serve to complement each other only if they really understand and appreciate each other. Both seek security, consistency, and fidelity in relationships, so there is a reasonably good chance that over time they will develop a greater appreciation for each other's opposite qualities.

CANCER-AQUARIUS (ouch!)

CANCER is more attached to family, more nostalgic, and more domestic than AQUARIUS. AQUARIUS is very friendly but not as emotionally involved with family and has much broader tastes and interests. CANCER, for example, becomes very emotionally attached to familiar surroundings and is inclined to live in one place for a long time. AQUARIUS, on the other hand, is more willing to follow whatever direction career changes and other demands necessitate. AQUARIUS quickly makes new friends and does not need as high a degree of intimacy as CANCER and, therefore, finds the transition to new surroundings much easier. CANCER is also more concerned with having financial and material security and is more inclined to worry if circumstances are not stable and secure. CANCER needs to be needed and wants a level of emotional bonding and nurturing that AQUARIUS may be incapable of.

CANCER-PISCES (excellent)

There is a tremendous flow of feeling, sympathy, and emotional rapport between these two, and they feel that their partner understands and empathizes with them in a way few others do. Both are sensitive, intuitive, receptive, and compassionate people who are easily moved by emotional appeals and needs of others. A deep mutual appreciation of music and the arts is also likely. There are differences between them: PISCES's sympathies are more broad and universal than CANCER's who is more concerned with family or others who are personally dear to CANCER. "Our family" or "our circle" matters more to CANCER than to PISCES, who treats friends and strangers equally. PISCES can be a little lax when it comes to remembering significant personal dates, like anniversaries or birthdays, whereas CANCER never is. Fortunately these differences are rather minor and unlikely to be much of problem between them.

CANCER-CANCER

Both are very sensitive, sympathetic and emotional with moods that shift and change like the tides. Though they may hide behind a shell, they are really very easily hurt and take almost everything personally. Both have deep feelings for and sentimental attachments to the past, home and family, or anything or anyone they once had a close affiliation with (school, home town, friends, etc.). If their backgrounds are very different, this may be more of a problem than it would be for other people, because their identification with their origins is so strong. Both need to be needed and desire a very close, secure, loving and protective relationship. Family or domesticity is extremely important to them. Because of their empathy for one another and their similar temperaments, they blend quite well together.

LEO

LEO-VIRGO

These two are very different! VIRGO is more modest, self-effacing, shy, and unobtrusive than LEO, who craves social approval, recognition, love, and applause. LEO tends to step into the limelight and outshine or overpower VIRGO. VIRGO is more emotionally self-sufficient than LEO is and may not give LEO all of the "strokes" and appreciation LEO wants. VIRGO also has a tendency to become fussy and particular, and these fits of perfectionism can have disastrous consequences when the target of VIRGO's critical eye is LEO. LEO is particularly sensitive to criticism and tends to interpret VIRGO's "constructive criticism" as a personal attack. VIRGO is more analytical and psychologically astute than LEO, who may not appreciate being "picked apart" or psychologically analyzed by VIRGO! Another problem in this relationship is that LEO may take for granted much of the work and assistance that VIRGO provides.

LEO-LIBRA

This can be a very warm and mutually fulfilling relationship. Both are romantics at heart and tend to be "in love with love." Both need and love romantic gestures, the giving and receiving of gifts, etc. Personal appearances and attractiveness is important to both of them as well, and both are somewhat vain. LEO is more decisive and very clear about personal preferences and desires while LIBRA is more flexible and will compromise graciously in order to please LEO. LEO is more self-absorbed or self-centered than LIBRA. Of the two of them, LEO is the stronger individual, and the balance of power in the relationship may be somewhat lopsided. However, LIBRA has a highly developed sense of fairness and equality and will protest sooner or later if LEO begins to expect obedience all of the time.

LEO-SCORPIO

Both are very proud, stubborn, strong-willed individuals and are attracted to the strength of character that they sense in each other. There is a feeling of conquest between them that may serve to intensify the excitement of their attraction to each other. However, their strong wills may also prove to be a problem in a long-term relationship. They face the possibility that their combined inflexibility will make it difficult for the two of them to reach mutually satisfying decisions because both tend to stubbornly resist compromising when their preferences are different. A battle of wills is likely to ensue! Another potential problem is jealousy or lopsided bonding. SCORPIO bonds very intensely in romantic relationships and is inclined towards monogamy. LEO is also very loyal but not nearly as intense, emotional, or obsessive as SCORPIO.

LEO-SAGITTARIUS (excellent)

Warmth, enthusiasm, vitality, and joy are kindled when these two are together, and there is great magnetism between them. SAGITTARIUS draws LEO out, evoking the more light-hearted, fun-loving side of LEO. SAGITTARIUS also keeps LEO from getting stuck in a rut by introducing new ideas and experiences that LEO enjoys. This is a mutually beneficial relationship which promises lots of good times and a very active life together. A downside is SAGITTARIUS's frequent indifference or obliviousness to others' personal feelings can result in blunt comments that wound LEOs easily hurt pride. LEO is also more loyal than SAGITTARIUS is, who tends to wander (in actuality and fantasy) more than LEO does.

LEO-CAPRICORN

CAPRICORN's more emotionally detached, reserved, down-to-earth and somewhat cynical or skeptical attitude contrasts with LEO's warm enthusiasm and basically cheerful temperament. Also, in their personal styles and tastes the differences are very apparent: CAPRICORN prefers the classics, simple elegance, and either a very conservative, traditional style or an austere less-is-more, keep-it-simple style. LEO has a generous, lavish hand and loves rich color, warmth, and brilliance that borders on gaudiness. Sometimes, this translates into emotional terms also. CAPRICORN is more careful, cooler, less inclined to gamble and wants a sure thing. LEO is more open, expressive and warm and needs an abundance of appreciation and affection—more than CAPRICORN is inclined to give sometimes. One thing they do have in common is they both take their commitments to heart and prize fidelity and loyalty.

LEO-AQUARIUS (complete opposites)

AQUARIUS is drawn to LEO's warmth and vitality, and LEO is drawn to AQUARIUS's uniqueness, intelligence, and savvy. There are significant differences between them though. AQUARIUS's colleagues, associates, and large social circle of friends and acquaintances are a very important part of AQUARIUS's life while AQUARIUS's need for close, personal relationships is not as great as LEO's. This characteristic is also reflected in their relationship! AQUARIUS may seem cool and aloof to LEO. From AQUARIUS's perspective, LEO takes life too personally and seems to dramatize events, idolize individuals, and, in general, be too self-absorbed. They are truly opposites in many ways and can certainly benefit from one another's attitudes and insights.

LEO-PISCES

A major difference between these is that PISCES lacks LEO's natural egocentricity, personal pride, ambition, and need to feel important and special. PISCES will not compete with LEO and is perfectly comfortable not being the one in the limelight. In fact, PISCES has a passive streak and tends to recede into the background, thus avoiding intensely competitive situations where decisiveness and aggressiveness are required. Personal recognition is not that important to PISCES. LEO, on the other hand, loves to be noticed, appreciated, the center of attention and tends to have an inflated sense of self-importance. PISCES is gentle, receptive, compassionate, and very sensitive to the emotional tone in any relationship. PISCES is attuned to the subtle signals and the unspoken feelings and needs of a partner while LEO is a bit vague when it comes to such things. If a partner wants or needs something from LEO, then they must clearly say so. PISCES's changeability, fluidity, elusiveness, sensitivity and awareness of subtlety fascinates or frustrates LEO, who is a much more straightforward, uncomplicated creature. Also, LEO can easily dominate or trample PISCES's feelings, and this can be the source of considerable unhappiness.

LEO-LEO

Both are proud, vibrant, warm but rather self-centered individuals. Both want to be the center of attention and may not want to share the starring role with their partner. For this relationship to work, neither can dominate. Instead, both must cooperate, which isn't something that comes naturally to either of them. Although it may not be obvious to others, both are very self-conscious individuals, who are very concerned with their personal creativity, personal recognition, and personal performance. Both are best suited to work that is very personal and creative; being an inconspicuous part of a large corporation is not for them. Their relationship is likely to be extraordinarily happy and fulfilling or else disastrous—no middle ground here. They tend to either adore each other or despise each other. They are both very loyal but must respect and believe in their partner. If they ever feel that their partner lacks integrity or honesty, is competing with them, or does not appreciate or understand their creative work and motivations, then the love and admiration that they have for each other turns sour quickly.

VIRGO

VIRGO-LIBRA

LIBRA loves company, can talk endlessly with friends and loves to hear others' experiences and thoughts on any subject. LIBRA is very accepting of different points of view and is disinclined to judge or even clearly evaluate what others say. VIRGO, on the other hand, loves to analyze and criticize and is intolerant of illogical or erroneous thinking. VIRGO is more demanding of others and confronts others when necessary. LIBRA finds these confrontations extremely uncomfortable and often embarrassing. VIRGO is much more exacting and demanding in all areas of life. At worst, VIRGO can view LIBRA as wishy-washy, and LIBRA can view VIRGO as prim and intolerant, but hopefully their appreciation of each other is much better than this! At best, their different natures can complement each other without annoying each other.

VIRGO-SCORPIO

Their essential natures are compatible, as both share a certain level of practicality, the need to analyze and dissect people and life, and a rather introspective approach to life's challenges. There are times, however, when SCORPIO strides fearlessly into a challenging situation, and VIRGO feels much more cautious and careful. SCORPIO may consider VIRGO to be too timid, and VIRGO may feel that SCORPIO lacks prudence. There are also many situations where SCORPIO is more stubborn and persevering than VIRGO. SCORPIO may view VIRGO's lack of commitment and dedication to a single purpose to be a sign of weakness. There is also the possibility that VIRGO will view SCORPIO as being a bit crude and too passionate or emotionally attached to certain situations or ideas. VIRGO has refined sensitivities and sometimes literally doesn't like to get "dirty hands" while SCORPIO is more primitive, raw, and not squeamish. Both need to strive to harmonize their different natures and not antagonize each other. The chances of doing so are very high because both sense in one another a generally compatible attitude towards life.

VIRGO-SAGITTARIUS

While VIRGO tends to focus on the trees, SAGITTARIUS is interested in the forest. Very often VIRGO points out problems with specific details of any situation while SAGITTARIUS would rather discuss the overall, general outlook rather than the practical details. These different approaches can balance each other. They are also likely to conflict with each other at times, especially when SAGITTARIUS feels that the details will take care of themselves, and VIRGO should simply have more faith in the process. VIRGO can be guilty of spending so much time criticizing the details that the overall goal of an otherwise excellent plan is missed. SAGITTARIUS, on the other hand, may need VIRGO's detailed analysis but not be willing to admit it. Positively, they can work together with SAGITTARIUS providing a great deal of vision and enterprise and VIRGO providing a great deal of practical advice, expertise, and skill. However, it is inevitable that SAGITTARIUS will feel annoyed with VIRGO's pettiness and criticism at times, and VIRGO will feel frustrated by SAGITTARIUS's sloppiness of thought or behavior. Much humor, tolerance, and awareness of their legitimate differences will be needed to work these problems through.

VIRGO-CAPRICORN (excellent)

Both are very practical, well-grounded people. They are responsible, trustworthy, and mature as well. CAPRICORN is a little more inclined to develop a strategic plan for success and a practical scheme for career advancement while VIRGO tends to rely more on practical skills and personal talents. VIRGO enjoys providing a clear, tangible service to others. The energies of these two blend well together, and they can be a very effective team in business affairs and practical undertakings. It is possible that their relationship will be a bit dry or mundane, particularly if the romantic and/or sexual connections are not very strong. The joy, color, and light side of life may be missing.

VIRGO-AQUARIUS

Although they approach problems and ideas from different perspectives, they have a good mental rapport. VIRGO focuses on specific details and prefers to specialize in a certain area while AQUARIUS takes a wider, more global view and looks for interrelationships in a large system without as much focus on any particular area of specialization. VIRGO is more concerned with effective and precise application of plans and helps AQUARIUS to apply ideas practically. They make a good team in social or intellectual pursuits. Their relationship may be a bit cool or formal, however, and hopefully there are other astrological factors to provide warmth, affection and romantic or sexual attraction.

VIRGO-PISCES

While VIRGO is very uncomfortable with ambiguity and is always categorizing and organizing life into clearly defined compartments, PISCES is quite content to absorb lots of seemingly contradictory ideas without having an urgent need to reconcile them. VIRGO likes to carve out an area of life, specialize in it, and develop skill and expertise in this well-defined domain whereas PISCES tends to drift among a wider variety of interests. VIRGO likes a neat, tidy, orderly environment whereas PISCES's natural habitat is cluttered, sloppy, even chaotic to an outside observer. PISCES is more poetic while VIRGO is more comfortable in the world of facts. Their differences do not necessarily conflict with one another, and there is a good possibility that they will appreciate and understand each other sufficiently to harmonize well. Neither are extremely ambitious or egocentric; both are gentle, even shy people, and their sensitivity is a plus in this relationship.

VIRGO-VIRGO

Both are prone to have fits of perfectionism, and at such times they are extremely critical and difficult to please. They may alternate between extreme neatness and sloppiness or be very particular about some things but very casual or even sloppy in handling other areas of life. Because both have an eye for detail and can be very skilled and exacting when they put their mind to it, they have the potential to work together very well in any area that requires extreme care and attention. There is the problem, however, that their combined perfectionism may make both dissatisfied with anything that they attempt. Both like to express their love for someone by doing practical things for that person, and both enjoy helping out with daily chores and various tasks. The similarity in their traits makes them a well-matched couple.

LIBRA

LIBRA-SCORPIO

In many situations, SCORPIO will respond with greater emotional intensity than LIBRA. While LIBRA is not a cool and aloof individual, SCORPIO's feelings can run deeper. For example, both want a close relationship, but SCORPIO can become intensely fixated on a person and possessive, whereas LIBRA maintains a sense of proportion and some reasonable degree of objectivity and emotional distance from others, even in marriage. SCORPIO's "urge to merge" can be very powerful. In general, LIBRA's approach to life tends to be more moderate and well-balanced while periodically SCORPIO tends to become intensely focused on some area of concern and even fanatical in pursuit of some interest. LIBRA's detached fairness can infuriate SCORPIO at times, and SCORPIO's inexplicable dark moods or fervent responses bewilder LIBRA. These differences need not create serious problems in their relationship. Emotional bonds between them can be very strong, especially if other astrological ingredients indicate strong romantic or sexual ties.

LIBRA-SAGITTARIUS

Both are outgoing, friendly people who enjoy socializing and delight in each other's company immensely. Very often SAGITTARIUS provides extra "zing" to the relationship with lots of grandiose ideas, dreams, visions, and restless wanderlust. LIBRA helps provide a more balanced, sensible perspective while usually being sympathetic to SAGITTARIUS as well. However, sometimes their joint activities may fail to be fruitful. LIBRA is often prone to go along with people even when there are lots of doubts. SAGITTARIUS may enthusiastically talk LIBRA into ventures that LIBRA should have the sense to question rather than meekly accept. Overall though, this is likely to be a most enjoyable relationship.

LIBRA-CAPRICORN

LIBRA is very social and prefers a lifestyle that involves lots of interaction with others. For example, a job that does not involve communication with others is very distasteful to LIBRA. CAPRICORN is more concerned with career, stature, and practical affairs than LIBRA, and many times LIBRA wishes that CAPRICORN would lighten up, take life less seriously, and simply be more fun to be with. CAPRICORN seems a little old-fashioned at times, too, which is frequently not agreeable with LIBRA. They can help complement each other with CAPRICORN contributing more to establishing a secure, well-founded plan for their lives and the future of their children (if they are married and have children) with LIBRA taking time to maintain social contacts and keep life in balance to make sure the pressures of work and other responsibilities do not become overwhelming. Pleasure and aesthetics are important to LIBRA but less so to CAPRICORN. Also, CAPRICORN tends to be autocratic while LIBRA is more democratic or egalitarian.

LIBRA-AQUARIUS (excellent)

Both are very social, active people. They are involved in community groups, and their lines of work probably bring them into contact with lots of people. They harmonize well with each other and are great friends. AQUARIUS is very attached to clubs, social groups, and colleagues. Sometimes LIBRA may feel that AQUARIUS needs friends more than a marriage partner or lover. In fact, LIBRA devotes much more attention to any close partnership. This difference in orientation is fairly subtle, however, and may not be a source of difficulty or conflict. Both tend to live in their minds and enjoy a partner who is awake and alive mentally—an intellectual peer. Fortunately, they have this in one another.

LIBRA-PISCES

Both are good listeners and receptive to others' points of view. They dislike having to engage in competitive behaviors or aggressive tactics in order to get their point across or receive fair treatment. Both appreciate that their partner shares their gentle attitude. LIBRA, however, may sometimes feel that PISCES is too gentle and receptive, as well as evasive or vague when asked questions and/or unable to be definite and articulate. LIBRA thrives on dialogue while PISCES often prefers to simply take in lots of ideas and ponder them for a long time before offering a point of view. LIBRA also has a strong sense of justice and equality and can be vengeful towards those who are seen as unjust while PISCES is more likely to feel compassion and sympathy even for those who are guilty.

LIBRA-LIBRA

Both invest enormous energy and time in personal relationships, for they both feel incomplete without a partner for companionship, conversation, and affection. They believe an experience isn't really satisfying unless it is SHARED. Both possess tact, diplomacy, charm, and a very strong desire for harmony in relationships. Furthermore, both tend to want to please everyone all of the time and to be liked by everyone; therefore, they often avoid taking strong, decisive stands or directly confronting thorny interpersonal problems. They want things to be nice, pretty, and pleasant, so they are likely to adapt their personal preferences or change their position to suit their partner. However, both also have a highly developed sense of fairness, balance, and proportion. Equality is very important to them and in this relationship (as perhaps in no other) they will certainly have an equal relationship with neither of them dominating. Beauty is very important to both of them so many of their discussions revolve around issues of taste and style.

SCORPIO

SCORPIO-SAGITTARIUS

These two individuals are different in many ways: very often, SAGITTARIUS feels lighthearted and enthusiastic about some idea, project, plan or dream and believes that SCORPIO is too stubborn to appreciate optimistic plans. Also, SAGITTARIUS loves festivities and socializing while SCORPIO often feels uncomfortable with large groups of people and prefers a deeper, more intimate involvement with just a few people rather than carousing with a large group. SCORPIO is capable of tremendous concentrated and persistent effort whereas SAGITTARIUS prefers to do a little bit of everything: traveling and developing a wide sphere of interests and activities rather than being limited to a few activities. Also, SCORPIO's feelings usually run much deeper than SAGITTARIUS's feelings, so SAGITTARIUS frequently fails to appreciate the depth of feeling that SCORPIO experiences. SCORPIO becomes very attached emotionally to a love partner and doesn't easily share SAGITTARIUS's attention and affection with anyone else. On the other hand, SAGITTARIUS is something of a flirt and may innocently arouse intense jealousy in SCORPIO. SAGITTARIUS can be weighed down by SCORPIO's suspiciousness, demands for loyalty and wholehearted involvement. Worse, SAGITTARIUS may simply ignore SCORPIO's needs and not realize how strongly SCORPIO feels. SAGITTARIUS has a much greater need for freedom. The two of them are so different that it will take a lot of compassion and understanding for them to be together for any length of time.

SCORPIO-CAPRICORN

Both are initially very careful about revealing feelings, motives and vulnerabilities; they are unwilling to reveal their inner core to others initially. It takes time for both of them to trust and become open emotionally. Both have a natural suspiciousness and reserve and are disinclined to have casual relationships. Some differences exist between them. For example, CAPRICORN has a much greater capacity for objectivity, emotional distance, and detachment than SCORPIO. CAPRICORN can be strangely aloof at times, especially when feeling threatened while SCORPIO will seethe with emotion. SCORPIO is instinctive and passionate and gets totally immersed in and attached to a lover. CAPRICORN may or may not feel as bonded, and even if CAPRICORN feels as strongly as SCORPIO, CAPRICORN may not be able to show the depth of feelings and emotional responsiveness that SCORPIO desires. This is unlikely to be a light, frothy, "fun" relationship, but then neither really wants that anyway.

SCORPIO-AQUARIUS

AQUARIUS is idealistic and can be very abstract and heady while SCORPIO relies more on instinct, intuitive sensitivity, and "gut feelings." SCORPIO's passions, irrational loves and hates, and intense emotional responses baffle AQUARIUS, who is far more rational and cerebral. More importantly, SCORPIO is very emotionally attached to a lover and can be become intensely fixated on a person. AQUARIUS is cool, unemotional, and rather aloof by comparison. AQUARIUS needs lots of friends and acquaintances but is not as involved in personal relationships as most people. This may create an emotional gap between them that may well be hard to reconcile. They are also both stubborn, rather opinionated, and inflexible. They'll need to appreciate and really understand the differences in their temperaments to harmonize in a long-term relationship.

SCORPIO-PISCES (excellent)

Both are very sensitive, feeling, compassionate people, and with one another they are able to have a depth of sharing, intimacy and emotional union that will find with few others. PISCES's sympathetic, non-judgmental, understanding attitude can be a healing balm to SCORPIO, who is more emotional and often carries secret guilt, inner conflicts, and pain. SCORPIO is more forceful than PISCES and will sometimes lash out with sarcasm or vindictiveness when hurt. This deeply wounds PISCES. PISCES is gentler, has less protective armor, and is generally more forgiving than SCORPIO.

Another difference in their natures is SCORPIO is highly sexual and physical while PISCES prefers more softness, subtlety, and romance. Basically however, they are quite compatible and can have a very fulfilling union.

SCORPIO-SCORPIO:

This partnership is an intense one, and they are likely to become very attached to or obsessed with each other. If romantic attraction is even reasonably strong, this relationship could easily lead to marriage. First of all, both are very marriage-oriented. It is difficult for them to be "just dating" someone because neither feel comfortable in light relationships. They prefer to either be wholeheartedly involved in a deep relationship or not at all. Both are also prone to be possessive and very emotionally attached to anyone that they give their love to. Like most lasting, important relationships, theirs will have its share of difficult times, for they both seem to thrive on passionate, tempestuous interactions. Stormy fights and sizzling reunions may typify their relationship. Both love intensely and hate with equal ferocity, so their relationship is likely to be either deeply satisfying or very destructive to both; there is no middle ground for these two!

SAGITTARIUS

SAGITTARIUS-CAPRICORN

Work versus play, or optimism and faith versus realism and doubt are likely to be issues in this relationship since SAGITTARIUS is the playful, optimistic one, and CAPRICORN is the realist. Many times SAGITTARIUS will be in the mood for socializing, traveling, or engaging in some form of entertainment while CAPRICORN feels that there are responsibilities that should be taken care of first. At such times CAPRICORN feels that SAGITTARIUS is too irresponsible, inconsiderate, and immature while SAGITTARIUS feels that CAPRICORN is boring and dull. SAGITTARIUS is also prone to fits of optimism and is inclined to gamble and speculate, whereas CAPRICORN prefers a well thought out, clear, practical plan. Also, CAPRICORN is inclined to be serious toward relationships and wants a secure, committed relationship while SAGITTARIUS wants more space and freedom. If their dissimilarities are not too extreme, they can complement rather than frustrate each other with SAGITTARIUS providing the energy and vision and CAPRICORN providing the steady hand and practical applications.

SAGITTARIUS-AQUARIUS

Outgoing and progressive, both enjoy busy lifestyles that keep them on the go. Both enjoy meeting new people, traveling, and keeping up with current events. Even later in life both will stay abreast of current trends in fashion, music, arts, literature, science, and politics. SAGITTARIUS tends to be a bit more philosophical than AQUARIUS, likes to have a sense of mission and purpose, and is sometimes prone to grandiose visions and exaggerated hopes. Neither are particularly sentimental, so their relationship may be very friendly but somewhat detached; fortunately this is not likely to be viewed as a problem by either of them. Both are independent and know that in this relationship they can have the space and freedom they need. Overall, their temperaments and interests are a bit different but blend well. This should be an enjoyable, interesting relationship.

SAGITTARIUS-PISCES

Both have strong imaginations and must have a dream to live for — without it the daily round of mundane existence would be too dull for either of them. Idealistic and romantic at heart, they sympathize with one another's hopes and dreams and what other people might call impractical fantasies. Both are essentially generous souls that dislike pettiness and limitations, such as budgets, diets, schedules, etc. There are many differences between them, though. PISCES is receptive and somewhat passive compared to SAGITTARIUS who has a lot of restless energy and more of a need to be physically active. Since SAGITTARIUS's energy level is usually higher than PISCES's, SAGITTARIUS can become impatient with PISCES's more relaxed pace. SAGITTARIUS is very straightforward while PISCES is more subtle and often evasive. Also, PISCES is very sensitive and would never make some of the blunt statements that SAGITTARIUS makes. SAGITTARIUS frequently wounds PISCES this way, quite unintentionally.

SAGITTARIUS-SAGITTARIUS

There is great camaraderie between these two. A love of traveling and a restless wanderlust are traits they have in common. Both are optimists and love to shoot for the stars. Minor details annoy them and pettiness is abhorrent to them. They have a youthful enthusiasm and a spirited, progressive outlook on life. With so much in common, they are able to have a wonderful time together. Neither takes life too seriously, so they can count on having a lively relationship with lots of variety, new adventure, and play. Both are also rather philosophical, so if they develop different philosophical or religious viewpoints, they may find it difficult to feel really close to each other! Also, both are often blunt, lacking in subtlety and frequently oblivious or indifferent to others' personal feelings. Fortunately, neither is insulted very easily. Overall, they are very well-matched in terms of temperaments and interests. They will be good pals if nothing else, and friendship is something both prize as much as romance.

CAPRICORN

CAPRICORN-AQUARIUS

Both invest a lot of time in work and career, and their talents and interests complement each other nicely. CAPRICORN brings practicality, objectivity, persistence, reliability, and tenacity while AQUARIUS brings greater ingenuity, sensitivity to current trends, an awareness of the complexities and intricacies inherent in any situation, and the ability to reach out to many people. A problem in their relationship is that it may become very focused on outer things and not enough on each other. If this occurs, they can become a bit detached and aloof from each other, and the domestic and romantic aspect of their relationship could weaken. Hopefully, both have other astrological factors (discussed elsewhere in this report) to provide warmth, emotional sensitivity, and romantic attraction in their relationship.

CAPRICORN-PISCES

These individuals are opposites in many respects. CAPRICORN is practical and realistic, deals effectively with the demands and responsibilities of the work place, and has a serious, sometimes cynical attitude toward life. PISCES, on the other hand, is a sensitive, imaginative dreamer at heart and far more emotional and empathic than CAPRICORN. PISCES intuitively knows that there is much more to life than what can be measured in material, concrete terms. CAPRICORN is essentially a "doubting Thomas" who requires proof. Where PISCES tends to be gullible, CAPRICORN tends to be skeptical. Also, CAPRICORN thrives on order and organization while PISCES is frequently disorganized or more comfortable in an atmosphere of clutter and "creative chaos." Both have a certain reserve, depth, and tendency to introspection and may have much to offer one another if they are willing to appreciate one another's differences.

CAPRICORN-CAPRICORN

Both are very practical, realistic people who set clear goals in life and are persistent, reliable workers that eventually reach a high level of success. Together they can build a secure and stable life. They appreciate the high level of integrity, maturity, and responsibility that they share with a partner. They could be a very successful team in business activities as well. A lack of zest and liveliness in their lives may develop, particularly if they have been married to each other for a long time. Both have a great deal of objectivity and emotional detachment, but this can degrade into the undesirable qualities of boredom, apathy, or heartlessness. If their relationship and lives become too filled with mundane concerns and too centered around responsibilities and business, they would greatly benefit by engaging in light, childish activities and amusements. This will restore them and make them more effective on the job. In fact, it would be a good idea if they made it a habit to remember to laugh heartily at least once a day; however, they might need a reminder to do this.

AQUARIUS

AQUARIUS-PISCES

Both are very open-minded and tolerant toward new ideas, the unusual, and the unconventional. AQUARIUS, however, is much more cerebral than PISCES, who is essentially intuitive and emotional. While AQUARIUS is cool, rational, and always able to give excellent reasons for an opinion or position, PISCES individuals are frequently unable to logically articulate their feelings, values and/or the subtleties that color and shape their attitudes or positions. Also, PISCES is a very sympathetic, compassionate person who feels the needs and pain of others very directly. AQUARIUS has a humanitarian outlook but is often more concerned with principles and ideals rather than with real people and their actual situations. In fact, AQUARIUS, is capable of considerable emotional detachment and objectivity unlike PISCES who is hopelessly subjective. AQUARIUS is uncomfortable with too much emotion and dependency, and PISCES may want more intimacy, affection, and emotional closeness than AQUARIUS wants or is capable of giving.

AQUARIUS-AQUARIUS

Both are active, outgoing people. It is likely that they live in an urban or suburban area. Neither cares to be at home most of the time. Both work effectively in large organizations and businesses. They are progressive and stay abreast of contemporary developments in politics, science and art. They have an excellent mental rapport and share intellectual interests or ideals that are very important to them. Their relationship, though very friendly, may lack warmth and depth of feeling. They may sometimes wonder whether they are comrades or lovers, for both can be rather impersonal at times so this quality may subtly permeate their relationship.

PISCES

PISCES-PISCES

Both possess great sensitivity, sympathy, imagination and intuition. They can communicate and understand one another at a very deep level, which is rare and very satisfying for both of them. Non-judgmental acceptance, tolerance, generosity, compassion, a love of beauty and peace—these are some of the positive qualities they share. They also have some less desirable qualities: passivity, hyper-sensitivity, a desire to escape rather than confront life and its challenges, and an inability to set boundaries or limits. Together they are likely to reinforce both the positive and negative potentials that both of them have.

Remember:

Even for one zodiac sign, there are multiple good and bad compatibilities, but if it's difficult to remember each specific combo, then go back to those four main elements: Fire, Earth, Air, and Water. Within the same element, signs are compatible (Air: Gemini, Libra, Aquarius are excellent), and some elements are good or bad with others: AIR + FIRE = GOOD; AIR + WATER = BAD; AIR + EARTH = BAD; FIRE + WATER = BAD; FIRE + EARTH = BAD; EARTH + WATER = GOOD. And remember, a sign directly next to your sign is a bad compatibility, most likely. However, this chapter only focused on SUN signs (personality), and therefore, is missing other essential ingredients like the Moon, Ascendant and planets, which may all be very compatible within a relationship, except for the Sun; thus making a great relationship. Just because one ingredient doesn't match up, does not mean you are doomed. It's important to look at the whole birth chart and the different combinations of compatible ingredients. Take a look below to check out all the matches within the 12 Sun signs.

ASTROLOGICAL ZODIAC SIGNS COMPATIBILITY GRID

Zodiac Signs	Aries	Taurus	Gemini	Cancer	Leo	Virgo	Libra	Scorpio	Sagittarius	Capricorn	Aquarius	Pisces
Aries	Superb Match	Many Conflicts	Can be Good	Tricky Pair	Superb Match	Tricky Pair	Can be Good	Difficult Match	Superb Match	Many Conflicts	Great Fun	Tricky Pair
Taurus	Many Conflicts	Superb Match	Tricky Pair	Good Match	Many Conflicts	Superb Match	Hard Work	Heaven or Hell	Opposite	Superb Match	Difficult Match	Good Match
Gemini	Can be Good	Tricky Pair	Superb Match	Not Suitable	Can be Good	Can be Good	Superb Match	Hard Work	Heaven or Hell	Difficult Match	Superb Match	Hard Work
Cancer	Tricky Pair	Good Match	Not Suitable	Superb Match	Difficult Match	Good Match	Not Suitable	Superb Match, Intense Passion	Difficult Match	Good Match	Steer Clear	Superb Match
Leo	Superb Match	Many Conflicts	Can be Good	Difficult Match	Superb Match	Many Conflicts	Good Match	Many Conflicts	Superb Match	Can be Good	Opposites	Can Work
Virgo	Tricky Pair	Superb Match	Can be Good	Good Match	Many Conflicts	Superb Match	Complement Each Other	Good Match	Difficult Match	Superb Match	Tricky Pair	Can be Good
Libra	Can be Good	Hard Work	Superb Match	Not Suitable	Good Match	Complement Each Other	Superb Match	Hard Work	Great Fun	Hard Work	Superb Match	Can be Good
Scorpio	Difficult Match	Heaven or Hell	Hard Work	Superb Match, Intense Passion	Many Conflicts	Good Match	Hard Work	Superb Match	Difficult Match	Great Fun	Steer Clear	Superb Match
Sagittarius	Superb Match	Opposite	Heaven or Hell	Difficult Match	Superb Match	Difficult Match	Great Fun	Difficult Match	Superb Match	Frustrating	Great Fun	Hard Work
Capricorn	Many Conflicts	Superb Match	Difficult Match	Good Match	Can be Good	Superb Match	Hard Work	Great Fun	Frustrating	Superb Match	Hard Work	Can be Good
Aquarius	Great Fun	Superb Match	Superb Match	Steer Clear	Opposites	Tricky Pair	Superb Match	Steer Clear	Great Fun	Hard Work	Superb Match	Tricky Pair
Pisces	Tricky Pair	Good Match	Hard Work	Superb Match	Can Work	Can be Good	Can be Good	Superb Match	Hard Work	Can be Good	Tricky Pair	Superb Match

My Story of Compatibilities

So why didn't it work out with that guy? You were attracted to him, but then he just seemed too needy and emotional. And why did he text all the time? It just moved too fast perhaps? Or maybe you just weren't compatible? Have you ever found yourself wondering about why things didn't work out? And I'm not even always referring to romantic relationships. We can apply these same questions to friendships, co-workers, and people we meet in our lives. How is it that certain people enter our lives, and we seem to just click while others we can't get away from fast enough or maybe can't even remember them days later? Thus, some people make no impression on you whatsoever while others may make a lifelong impression. Have you ever thought about this? Okay, so I have. Maybe I have too much time on my hands, but I also find myself continually fascinated by how we interact with individuals in our lives.

I asked my ex-boyfriend once to think of all the women he's dated and name their birthdays: January 28, February 4, February 16 (me) and February 1. Doesn't it seem odd he dated only Aquarian women in his lifetime? And he was a LIBRA. Yes, Libra's most compatible sign is Aquarius, probably more so than a Gemini. Also, he was currently interested in dating a girl with a birthday of May 28, a Gemini.

So I also did this little experiment with myself (and I challenge you to do the same!) and tallied up all my ex-boyfriend's birthdays and found it quite telling really. My first boyfriend in high school was a VIRGO. Well, that's not very compatible with an AQUARIUS, but his MOON sign was LIBRA, which explains some compatibility. My second boyfriend was a CANCER! Wait! What?? How did that one happen? Well, it only lasted three months—he was emotional, clingy, insecure, and mostly, just plain old manipulative. Not saying CANCERS always have those traits, but some may. He definitely didn't allow me to be me and to give me the freedom that I so desperately searched for at the age of 22. My third boyfriend is the LIBRA I mentioned earlier. His Moon was VIRGO (he was much more grounded than me) and his Ascendant was AQUARIUS. We talked for hours (communication is key for AIR Signs), and I found him to be very fascinating and intelligent, all key ingredients for Aquarians' mate selection criteria.

I also dated a VIRGO at the age of 29, but there was something missing from our relationship. We talked a lot, which I love, but it was like we were talking on different dimensions; I can't quite explain it. He was crazy about me, texted me, called me way too much, and even after I told him numerous times, I needed my space. That ended quickly. His Moon sign was a TAURUS, I later found out. Thus, it would NEVER work. We just existed in different worlds.

I once tried dating one of my best guy friends. He and I seemed somewhat compatible, so we tried dating. He was a PISCES/ARIES cusp, and oh boy, did he ever represent that! I loved his "manliness." You find that in an ARIES—but my personality walked all over his PISCES (sensitive and caring) demeanor and that ended within weeks. He and I still remain good friends today. I gave him the Facebook Challenge, and he kept reading off all his friends' birthdays listed on Facebook and they were all LEOs. Yes, ARIES's best compatibility is a LEO. I slowly convinced all my exes about the zodiac compatibilities!

And is it weird that when my friends want to set me up with people, my first thought/question is "What's their birthday?"

Two years ago, a friend set me up with an Aquarius male, so I said, "Why not? At least he'll be compatible in some sense."

The first date went well, we talked a lot (a common ingredient among AIR signs), and I later discovered he had a LIBRA moon. I was convinced he had some EARTH elements in him though (he seemed very grounded and practical), so I later discovered that his Ascendant sign was TAURUS. We were very compatible and are now married! Thus, I encourage you to "Zodiac Stalk" your potential interests or dating partners now because you just never know!

I keep saying that astrology has to be more than just a coincidence ... but do coincidences really happen?

Many people say, "There is no such thing as a coincidence and that everything happens for a reason."

But what are the odds that the majority of the people that are in your life at this very moment have a certain birthday? Do birthdays really matter? If we had this information (and it held water, meaning there was more to it), maybe we'd have fewer people getting married to the wrong people, and even as far as to say that maybe we'd lower the chances of divorce. This could save us all thousands of dollars. Did you know that on average in the US the cost of a wedding today is about $27,000, and the cost of divorce is approximately $30,000?

So save yourself some money and time and ask one simple question the next time you meet a potential new romantic partner, "Hey, what's your birthday?"

HOMEWORK

Did you know that on Facebook you can tally up all your friends' birthdays into a histogram (http://www.facebookspectrum.com/)? Then you can discover who the majority of your friends are based on their zodiac signs. So, are you compatible? I asked my ex-boyfriend to try this using his Facebook friends. I guessed the month with his most friends—February—and I was right. He's a LIBRA and his most compatible sign is an AQUARIUS (which is mostly February). He then asked me to predict the month with his fewest friends, and I guessed July, which is mostly CANCER. I was right again. Based on zodiac signs, I predicted, who he was and wasn't friends with – a CANCER and a LIBRA are not compatible.

Quickly, two issues come to mind with this approach:

1. Everyone who is a Facebook friend isn't really a "great" friend—some are acquaintances, and some are just people you barely know. Thus it might not be a great dataset to test this theory on, but it's worth a try; and

2. Obviously the birthday months do not represent zodiac signs since zodiacs are from mid-month to mid-month. Again, it can be misleading; however, the fact that I was able to predict which months my ex had more friends in than others may attest to the zodiac compatibility idea. But read on more to decide for yourself and go try the Facebook Challenge!

HOMEWORK

I encourage you to "Zodiac Stalk" your potential love interests. Just ask what their birthday is! Remember that you need to ask about their date, time, and location!

Chapter 4
Other Important Ingredients

1 Cup Personality

½ Cup Numerology

½ Cup Chinese Zodiacs

¾ Cup Love Language

This chapter is dedicated to adding other ingredients—like chocolate chips or the vanilla in a chocolate chip cookie recipe—that are intertwined in our culture, and that are just as important as our zodiac ingredients. These include personality tests (specifically the Myers-Briggs personality test), numerology, Eastern ideas such as Chinese astrology, and our love languages (by Gary Chapman). Most people who discuss zodiacs do so from one perspective, but my goal in the past year was to use a recipe to truly understand people and their relationships. You can't make cake or cookies with just flour. You need all the other essential ingredients, such as eggs, sugar, and butter. This is the same thing. We need zodiacs, personality, numerology, Chinese zodiacs and love languages to begin to fully discover ourselves and the relationships we have with those around us. Here are my thoughts on the matters. Again, I'm no expert, but I did my research.

1 Cup PERSONALITY

The Myers-Briggs Type Indicator (MBTI) assessment is a psychometric questionnaire designed to measure psychological preferences in how people perceive the world and make decisions. The original developers of the personality inventory were Katharine Cook Briggs and her daughter, Isabel Briggs Myers. The MBTI has been called "the world's most widely used personality assessment" with as many as 2,000,000 assessments administered annually. However, some academic psychologists have criticized the MBTI instrument, claiming that it "lacks convincing validity data." So the basis behind this most popular personality test—basically, why I am bringing this up—is that if our society strongly believes in an instrument, such as this one which has little validity, then why can't we give zodiacs and astrology some credit? My point is astrology is another essential ingredient we must utilize in understanding ourselves. Here is the list of Myers-Briggs personality types, essentially sixteen types of personalities. Take a look at these types and their descriptions and decide which one/s most clearly describe you. Then go to this website http://www.humanmetrics.com/cgi-win/jtypes2.asp) to figure out where you stand by answering the questions:

ISTJ—The Duty Fulfillers: Quiet, serious, earn success by thoroughness and dependability. Practical, matter-of-fact, realistic, and responsible. Decide logically what should be done and work toward it steadily, regardless of distractions. Take pleasure in making everything orderly and organized—their work, their home, their life. Value traditions and loyalty. Estimated to be 7-10% of the American population.

ESTJ—The Guardians: Practical, realistic, matter-of-fact. Decisive, quickly move to implement decisions. Organize projects and people to get things done. Focus on getting results in the most efficient way possible. Take care of routine details. Have a clear set of logical standards, systematically follow them and want others to do so also. Forceful in implementing their plans. Estimated to be 12-15% of the American population.

ISFJ—The Nurturers: Quiet, friendly, responsible, and conscientious. Committed and steady in meeting their obligations. Thorough, painstaking, and accurate. Loyal, considerate, notice and remember specifics about people who are important to them. Concerned with how others feel. Strive to create an orderly and harmonious environment at work and at home. Estimated to be 7-10% of the American population.

ESFJ—The Caregivers: Warmhearted, conscientious, and cooperative. Want harmony in their environment; work with determination to establish it. Like to work with others to complete tasks accurately and on time. Loyal, follow through even in small matters. Notice what others need in their day-by-day lives and try to provide it. Want to be appreciated for who they are and for what they contribute. Estimated to be 11-14% of the American population. This is my personality (majority of the time).

ISTP—The Mechanics: Tolerant and flexible. Quiet observers until a problem appears, then act quickly to find workable solutions.

Analyze what makes things work and readily get through large amounts of data to isolate the core of practical problems. Interested in cause and effect, organize facts using logical principles Value efficiency. Estimated to be 4-7% of the American population.

ESTP—The Doers: Flexible and tolerant, they take a pragmatic approach focused on immediate results. Theories and conceptual explanations bore them—they want to act energetically to solve the problem. Focus on the here-and-now, spontaneous, enjoy each moment that they can be active with others. Enjoy material comforts and style. Learn best through doing. Estimated to be 6-8% of the American population.

ESFP—The Performers: Outgoing, friendly, and accepting. Exuberant lovers of life, people, and material comforts. Enjoy working with others to make things happen. Bring common sense and a realistic approach to their work and make work fun. Flexible and spontaneous, adapt readily to new people and environments. Learn best by trying a new skill with other people. Estimated to be 8-10 % of the American population.

ISFP—The Artists: Quiet, friendly, sensitive, and kind. Enjoy the present moment, what's going on around them. Like to have their own space and to work within their own time frame. Loyal and committed to their values and to people who are important to them. Dislike disagreements and conflicts, do not force their opinions or values on others. Estimated to be 5-7% of the American population.

ENTJ—The Executives: Frank, decisive, assume leadership readily. Quickly see illogical and inefficient procedures and policies, develop and implement comprehensive systems to solve organizational problems. Enjoy long-term planning and goal setting. Usually well-informed, well-read, enjoy expanding their knowledge and passing it on to others. Forceful in presenting their ideas. Estimated to be 3-5% of the American population.

INTJ—The Scientists: Have original minds and great drive for implementing their ideas and achieving their goals. Quickly see patterns in external events and develop long-range explanatory perspectives. When committed, organize a job and carry it through. Skeptical and independent, have high standards of competence and performance—for themselves and others. Estimated to be 1-2% of the American population.

ENTP—The Visionaries: Quick, ingenious, stimulating, alert, and outspoken. Resourceful in solving new and challenging problems.

Adept at generating conceptual possibilities and then analyzing them strategically. Good at reading other people. Bored by routine, will seldom do the same thing the same way, apt to turn to one new interest after another. Estimated to be 4-6% of the American population.

INTP—The Thinkers: Seek to develop logical explanations for everything that interests them. Theoretical and abstract, interested more in ideas than in social interaction. Quiet, contained, flexible, and adaptable. Have unusual ability to focus in depth to solve problems in their area of interest. Skeptical, sometimes critical, always analytical. Estimated to be 3-4% of the American population.

ENFJ—The Givers: Warm, empathetic, responsive, and responsible. Highly attuned to the emotions, needs, and motivations of others. Find potential in everyone, want to help others fulfill their potential. May act as catalysts for individual and group growth. Loyal, responsive to praise and criticism. Sociable, facilitate others in a group, and provide inspiring leadership. Estimated to be 3-5% of the American population.

INFJ—The Protectors: Seek meaning and connection in ideas, relationships, and material possessions. Want to understand what motivates people and are insightful about others. Conscientious and committed to their firm values. Develop a clear vision about how best to serve the common good. Organized and decisive in implementing their vision. Estimated to be 1-2% of the American population.

ENFP—The Inspirers: Warmly enthusiastic and imaginative. See life as full of possibilities. Make connections between events and information very quickly and confidently proceed based on the patterns they see. Want a lot of affirmation from others and readily give appreciation and support. Spontaneous and flexible, often rely on their ability to improvise and their verbal fluency. Estimated to be 6-7% of the American population.

INFP—The Idealists: Idealistic, loyal to their values and to people who are important to them. Want an external life that is congruent with their values. Curious, quick to see possibilities, can be catalysts for implementing ideas. Seek to understand people and to help them fulfill their potential. Adaptable, flexible, and accepting unless a value is threatened. Estimated to be 3-4% of the American population.

What's great about the Myers-Briggs typologies is that it discusses compatibilities. Read more at: http://www.personalitypage.com/html/type_to_type.html). When researchers Tieger and Barron-

Tieger examined couples on these typologies (see the grid below), they found that, in general, more similar couples experienced a higher rate of satisfaction with their partner, which has been found in most research ("birds of a feather flock together"). However, there were some combinations that worked well despite having few things in common and some pairings of similar partners that weren't quite so successful—just like zodiac compatibilities.

MYERS-BRIGGS PERSONALITY COMPATIBILITY GRID

	ISTJ	ESTJ	ISFJ	ESFJ	ISTP	ESTP	ESFP	ISFP	ENTJ	INTJ	ENTP	INTP	ENFJ	INFJ	ENFP	INFP
ISTJ	Great Match	Difficult Match	Okay	Okay	Difficult Match	Great Match	Great Match	Benefit	Unstable	Boring	Mentor	Benefit	Great Match	Hard Work	Worst	Okay at First
ESTJ	Unstable	Great Match	Okay	Okay	Great Match	Difficult Match	Benefit	Mentor	Boring	Difficult Match	Benefit	Benefit	Great Match	Hard Work	Great Match	Okay at Worst
ISFJ	Okay	Okay	Great Match	Unstable	Benefit	Great Match	Great Match	Match	Difficult Match	Great Match	Hard Work	Worst	Okay at First	Difficult Match	Mentor	Benefit
ESFJ	Okay	Okay	Unstable	Great Match	Mentor	Benefit	Difficult Match	Match	Great Work	Hard Match	Great First	Good at Worst	Boring	Difficult Match	Benefit	Great Match
ISTP	Difficult Match	Great Match	Benefit	Mentor	Great Match	Unstable	Difficult Match	Boring	Match	Benefit	Okay	Okay	Okay at Worst	First	Hard Match	Work
ESTP	Great Match	Difficult Match	Great Match	Benefit	Unstable	Great Match	Great Boring	Match	Difficult Benefit	Mentor	Okay	Okay	Okay at First	Worst	Hard Work	Great Match
ESFP	Great Match	Match	Great Benefit	Difficult Match	Difficult Match	Match	Great Match	Boring	Great Match	Unstable	Hard First	Worst	Great Work	Match	Benefit	Okay Mentor
ISFP	Benefit	Mentor	Difficult Match	Great Match	Boring	Match	Unstable	Great Match	Great Worst	Good at First	Great Match	Hard Work	Great Match	Difficult Benefit	Okay	Okay
ENTJ	Match	Boring	Great Match	Great Work	Difficult Match	Great Benefit	Great Match	Great Match	Great Match	Good at Match	Great Match	Difficult Match	Great Okay	Okay	Benefit	Mentor
INTJ	Boring	Difficult Match	Hard Work	Great Match	Benefit	Mentor	Worst	First	Good at Unstable	Great Match	Great Match	Difficult Match	Okay	Okay	Match	Great Benefit
ENTP	Mentor	Benefit	Great Worst	Okay at First	Okay	Alike	Hard Work	Great Match	Great Match	Difficult Match	Great Match	Great Match	Great Unstable	Benefits	Great Match	Difficult Match
INTP	Benefit	Great Match	Great First	Okay at Worst	Okay	Okay	Great Okay	Match	Hard Match	Great Match	Great Unstable	Great Match	Great Mentor	Benefit	Difficult Match	Boring
ENFJ	Great Match	Hard Work	Difficult Match	Boring	Worst	Okay at Match	Benefit	Great Match	Great Okay	Okay	Great Benefit	Mentor	Great Match	Unstable	Difficult Match	Great Match
INFJ	Hard Work	Great Match	Boring	Difficult Match	Okay at First	Worst	Mentor	Benefit	Okay	Okay	Great Match	Benefit	Difficult Unstable	Great Match	Great Match	Difficult Match
ENFP	Worst	Great First	Mentor	Benefit	Great Match	Hard Work	Okay	Okay	Benefit	Great Match	Boring	Great Match	Difficult Match	Difficult Match	Great Match	Great Unstable
INFP	Okay at First	Worst	Benefit	Great Match	Hard Work	Great Match	Okay	Okay	Mentor	Benefit	Difficult Match	Boring	Great Match	Great Match	Unstable	Great Match

Remember:

Even though the Myers-Briggs personality test is not a Zodiac element, I still think it's important to know yours and your partner's in order to see if you are compatible. Plus, it's another ingredient that could explain a lot about you, and/or your relationship. Numerology is next, which is based on numbers, obviously, of your birth date, and is commonly associated with Zodiac signs.

1/2 Cup Numerology

Numerology is the study of numbers and the occult manner in which they reflect certain aptitudes and character tendencies as an integral part of the cosmic plan. Each number has a numeric value that provides a related cosmic vibration. You can discover your number by adding the sum of the numbers in your birth date. There are eleven numbers used in constructing numerology charts. These numbers are 1, 2, 3, 4, 5, 6, 7, 8, 9, 11, and 22. Larger numbers that occur from adding the numbers in the complete birth date are reduced by adding the digits together until the sum achieved is one of the core numbers. Merely add the components of the larger number together (repeatedly, if necessary) until a single digit (or the "master" numbers 11 or 22) results. It is easy to calculate. Simply add the digits of your birth data and keep "reducing" (explained via the example here) to a single digit. Note it as follows: Birth Month is February, which is the 2nd month = 2; Birth Day is 16 = 16; Birth Year is 1981 = 1981. Add up the digits of all of these numbers: 2+1+6+1+9+8+1 =28. Further "reduce" this number to a single digit by adding its digits: 2+8 = 10. And then further reduce it if necessary: 1+0 = 1. The final digit, 1, is the Birth Path Number! Each of these numbers represents different characteristics and expressions (find more information at: http://www.cafeastrology.com /numerology.html and http://www.astrology-numerology.com /num-relationship.html):

- #1: One is a leader and indicates the ability to stand alone. Keywords: independent, creative, original, ambitious, determined, self-assured. If expressed negatively: arrogant, stubborn, impatient, and self-centered. As lovers, they take the lead in love; love and/or the chase is of utmost importance to these lovers. There can be self-centeredness, however. These lovers are willing to experiment, and they can be quite exciting—they also require a lot of excitement because they can become bored easily. Most like a LEO.

- #2: This is the mediator and peace-lover and indicates the desire for harmony. It is a gentle, considerate, and sensitive vibration. Keywords: diplomatic, warm, peaceful, sensitive. If expressed negatively: too dependent, manipulative, passive-aggressive. As lovers: will bend over backwards to keep a relationship running smoothly. They offer emotional security to their lovers. It is associated with the Moon, and since the Moon rules Cancer in astrology, 2 is similar to the CANCER vibration.

- #3: Three is a sociable, friendly, and outgoing vibration. Kind, positive, and optimistic, they enjoy life and have a good sense of humor. Keywords: jovial, friendly, positive, adventurous, self-expressive. If expressed negatively: extravagant, scattered, and superficial. As lovers, they are fun, energetic, and willing to experiment. These lovers need space and contact with others in order to feel content. If they feel confined, they will be unhappy and restless. Allowed the freedom to socialize and scatter their energies, they are exciting and happy lovers. Most like a SAGITTARIUS.

- #4: This is the worker. Practical with a love of detail, they are trustworthy, hard-working, and helpful. Keywords: steady, logical, self-disciplined, problem-solving. If expressed negatively: contrary, stubborn, and narrow-minded. Although steady and generally trustworthy as lovers, they can be quite emotional and frustrated if they feel caged in. They tend to need some level of confrontation in their love lives. A relationship that stagnates will bring out their contrary nature. They love to solve problems, and if allowed to "take on" and tackle predicaments, they are very loyal lovers. Most like a VIRGO or TAURUS.

- #5: This is the freedom lover and is an intellectual vibration. These are "idea" people with a love of variety and the ability to adapt to most situations. Keywords: adaptable, freedom-loving, romantic, resourceful, witty, fun-loving, curious, flexible, accommodating. If expressed negatively: non-committal, irresponsible, inconsistent. These lovers are generally attractive to the opposite sex because they are adaptable, curious, and friendly. Their wit and love of fun is unmistakable. In order to be happy in love, they need some level of change and variety. They also require mental stimulation. They are quick to adapt to ups and downs, but when under-stimulated, they can be inconsistent and resist making commitments. Most like a GEMINI.

- #6: This is the peace lover and is a loving, stable, and harmonious vibration. Keywords: compassionate, stable, family-loving, trustworthy, domesticated. If expressed negatively: superficial, jealous, possessive, and unwilling to change. Generally, they have a deep dislike of discord and will generally work hard at keeping the peace. They are very attached to their homes and their families. At their best, they are devoted and stable partners who do whatever they can to maintain balance and harmony. At their worst, they take their peace-loving natures too far and become lethargic, diplomatic to the point of superficiality, and jealous. Most like a LIBRA.

- #7: This is the deep thinker and is a spiritual vibration. These people are not very attached to material things and are introspective and generally quiet. Keywords: unusual, introspective, intuitive, psychic, wise, reserved. If expressed negatively: melancholic, odd, leaves too much to chance, hard to reach. As lovers they are a little spaced out and sometimes hard to reach and to understand. However, their disinterest in material things and focus on spirituality makes them an interesting bed partner and mate. They are intuitive, and some are psychic. Although they can be loners at different times in their lives, they are often devoted partners. They can reach levels of intimacy and romance beyond many people's imaginations. However, their goals in love may be too lofty, and thus they can be prone to disappointment when relationships inevitably fall short of ideal. Most like a PISCES.

- #8: This is the manager and is a strong, successful, and material vibration. Keywords: ambitious, business-minded, practical, leading, authoritative, successful, courageous, accomplished, organized. If expressed negatively: tense, narrow, materialistic, and forceful. As lovers they take a commitment with responsibility and bravery. When they treat relationships like business deals, however, they can easily alienate partners and fall short of creating a tolerant and romantic atmosphere. Eights are generally practical and secure and offer their mates stability and security. Most like a CAPRICORN.

- #9: This is the teacher and is a tolerant, somewhat impractical, and sympathetic vibration. Keywords: jack of all trades, humanitarian, sympathetic, helpful, emotional, tolerant, active, determined. If expressed negatively: financially careless, moody, bullying, overly emotional, sullen, and restless. As lovers they are involved and helpful. Because they are sympathetic, they can easily be doormats. They show their love by helping their partners and assuming their lovers' problems. If triggered, their emotions can be volcanic, and a seemingly meek personality can resort to bullying tactics when unhappy. Most like a SCORPIO.

- #11: This is the giver and innovator with an unmistakable streak of humanitarianism. Keywords: idealistic, intuitive, considerate, tolerant, accepting, steadfast. If expressed negatively: too dependent, over-sensitive, and manipulative. As lovers they are romantic in the idealistic sense of the word. They want to see good in people, and they find it. Elevens are the least selfish lovers, and they are extremely considerate. They won't push you to do anything. They hold onto their partners (and their friends), and they are the masters of compromise. Elevens are tolerant and accepting. Most like an AQUARIUS.

- #22: This is the master builder. Although number twenty-twos are idealists and visionaries, they still manage to keep their feet on the ground. Keywords: achiever, wise, intense, idealistic, resourceful, passionate. If expressed negatively: overly emotional, destructive, and dramatic. As lovers, it's all or nothing. They don't seem capable of doing things halfway, and that includes their relationships. They are generally bent on achieving in life, and their sheer intensity is something people either love or hate. Most like a LEO.

Remember:

Your numerology number represents eleven different types of people, similar to the Zodiac signs, and can explain different characteristics about a person (based on their birth date). In addition, you can use the birth name—the name given a person at birth—to determine the Name Number (also known as the Expression Number), which reveals the overall personality. However, this has little to do with your birth date, so I'm not going to go into this further, but you can read much more about this online (http://www.tokenrock.com/numerology/ expression_number.php).

NUMEROLOGY COMPATIBILITY GRID

	Easy compatibility or seem to be a natural fit	Compatible/find it easy to get along.	Neutral	A challenge--much compromise required
1	1, 5, 7	3, 9	8	2, 4, 6
2*	2, 4, 8	3, 6	9	1, 5, 7
3	3, 6, 9	1, 2, 5		4, 7, 8
4*	2, 4, 8	6, 7		1, 3, 5, 9
5	1, 5, 7	3, 9	8	2, 4, 6
6	3, 6, 9	2, 4, 8		1, 5, 7
7	1, 5, 7	4	9	2, 3, 6, 8
8	2, 4, 8	6	1, 5	3, 7, 9
9	3, 6, 9	1, 5	2, 7	4, 8

*Note: For the purposes of evaluating relationships, master numbers 11 and 22 are reduced to 2 and 4 respectively.

1/2 Cup Chinese Zodiac Sign

Chinese astrology (see http://www.gotohoroscope.com/chinese-astrology/) is probably the oldest method and it is based on many things including animals, elements and the symbols of Ying (the Sun) and Yang (the Moon). Ancient astrologists describe the characteristics of twelve creatures and use these personality traits to make up the main formation of an astrological calendar. In Chinese astrology, each animal represents a year of birth and those people born in that period are believed to acquire some of the designated animal's character. They additionally obtain an association with Wood, Fire, Earth, Metal or Water and will also be thought of as a Ying or Yang person. Utilizing both Chinese and Western methods of thinking together can reveal a much clearer and fuller picture of your recipe. It can help differentiate and explain why two people of the same sign have differing qualities in varying strengths. The influence from the Chinese animals often adds a little extra to our personalities (about ½ cup!). The correlation of Chinese and Western horoscopes is very useful information to examine for the purpose of a personality interpretation. Most people are aware of their Western sun sign and will recognize their similarity to the average assumed traits. While this gives a fairly accurate portrayal, it can sometimes leave out the finer and more significant details of a person's temperament. In order to fully assess someone's zodiac recipe, we need to look beyond the Western horoscope (i.e., Sun sign) and into the deeper theories of the centuries old Chinese doctrines.

Identifying the Chinese zodiac reflects several similarities to the Western zodiac. Both have time cycles divided into twelve parts (the majority of those parts with names of animals), and each is widely associated with a person's personality. Nevertheless, there are major differences. The Chinese 12-part cycle corresponds to years rather than months. The Chinese zodiac is represented by twelve animals whereas some of the signs in the Western zodiac are not animals, despite the implication of the Greek etymology of "zodiac." The animals of the Chinese zodiac are not associated with constellations, let alone those spanned by the ecliptic plane. These are easier to discover because they are based on the year you were born, and are listed below (with their positive and negative characteristics), along with the equivalent Western zodiac sign.

See below for dates or go online and check your own Chinese Zodiac (http://www.travelchinaguide.com/intro/social_customs/zodiac/).

Rat: Positive: charming, protective, compassionate, communicative, dynamic, familial, thrifty, skillful, attractive, idealistic, prosperous, experimental, calm, sensual, loving, talented, adaptable, open-minded, and brilliant entrepreneurs. Negative: possessive, picky, defensive, excessive, addictive, fickle, stingy, bossy, exploitive, anxious, argumentative, opinionated, overbearing, and self-obsessed. Equivalent Western Sign is **Sagittarius**.

Years of the Rat

02/18/1912–02/05/1913	02/05/1924–01/23/1925	01/24/1936–02/10/1937
02/10/1948–01/28/1949	01/28/1960–02/14/1961	02/15/1972–02/02/1973
02/02/1984–02/19/1985	02/19/1996–02/06/1997	02/06/2008–01/25/2009

Ox: Positive: patient, contemplative, skillful, eloquent, confident, familiar, authoritative, industrious, and sure of foot. Negative:

The Zodiac Recipe

prejudice, chauvinistic, proud, tyrannical, petty, critical, eccentric, bigoted, conservative, grumpy, and on occasion, violent. Equivalent Western sign is **Capricorn**.

Years of the Ox

02/06/1913-01/25/1914	01/24/1925-02/12/1926	02/11/1937-01/30/1938
01/29/1949-02/16/1950	02/15/1961-02/04/1962	02/03/1973-01/22/1974
02/20/1985-02/08/1986	02/07/1997-01/27/1998	01/26/2009-02/13/2010

Tiger: Positive: lovable, alluring, warm-hearted, altruistic, honorable, hard-working, pleasant, independent, engaging, dynamic, and idealistic sweetie pies. Negative: rash, hotheaded, reckless, infatuated, quarrelsome, caustic, moody, predatory, rebellious, disobedient, and irreverent rascals. Equivalent Western sign is **Aquarius**.

Years of the Tiger

01/26/1914-02/13/1915	02/13/1926-02/01/1927	01/31/1938-02/18/1939
02/17/1950-02/05/1951	02/05/1962-01/24/1963	01/23/1974-02/10/1975
02/09/1986-01/28/1987	01/28/1998-02/15/1999	02/14/2010-02/02/2011

Rabbit: Positive: sensitive, tactful, home-loving, refined, prudent, discreet, long-living, ambitious, cultured, well-mannered, artistic, considerate, scholarly, suave, graciously hospitable, modest, and unimpeachably virtuous. Negative: snobbish, secretive, pedantic, complicated, haughtily indifferent, self-indulgent, hypochondriac, punctilious, judgmental, self-righteous, deceptive, self-centered, and terminally condescending. Equivalent Western sign is **Pisces**.

Years of the Rabbit

02/14/1915– 02/02/1916	02/02/1927– 01/22/1928	02/19/1939– 02/08/1940
02/06/1951– 01/26/1952	01/25/1963– 02/12/1964	02/11/1975– 01/30/1976
01/29/1987– 02/16/1988	02/16/1999– 02/04/2000	02/03/2011– 01/22/2012

Dragon: Positive: vibrant, magnanimous, charismatic, principled, self-sufficient, discriminating, compelling, sentimental, accomplished, noble-hearted, healthy, and prodigiously shrewd. Negative: bombastic, dissatisfied, ruthless, demanding, opinionated, mawkish, egocentric, defensive, power-mad, foolhardy, willful, and pompous. Equivalent Western Sign is **Aries**.

Years of the Dragon

02/03/1916– 01/22/1917	01/23/1928– 02/09/1929	02/09/1940– 01/26/1941
01/27/1952– 02/13/1953	02/13/1964– 02/01/1965	01/31/1976– 02/17/1977
02/17/1988– 02/05/1989	02/05/2000– 01/23/2001	01/23/2012– 02/09/2013

Snake: Positive: amiable, compromising, fun loving, altruistic, honorable, sympathetic, philosophical, charitable, a paragon of fashion, intuitive, discreet, diplomatic, amusing, and sexy. Negative: self-righteous, imperious, judgmental, conniving, mendacious, grabby, clingy, pessimistic, fickle, haughty, ostentatious, and a very sore loser. Equivalent Western sign is **Taurus**.

Years of the Snake

01/23/1917– 02/10/1918	02/10/1929– 01/29/1930	01/27/1941– 02/14/1942
02/14/1953– 02/02/1954	02/02/1965– 01/20/1966	02/18/1977– 02/06/1978
02/06/1989– 01/26/1990	01/24/2001– 02/11/2002	02/10/2013– 01/30/2014

Horse: Positive: productive, enthusiastic, amusing, warm-hearted, talented, agreeable, industrious, generous, sociable, autonomous, strong minded, sexy, curious, persuasive, and logical. Negative: defiant, condescending, unscrupulous, anxious, moody, excessively pragmatic, opportunistic, hard-nosed, self-serving, and so obtuse as to seem to have gone both blind and deaf at once. Equivalent Western sign is **Gemini**.

Years of the Horse

02/11/1918– 01/31/1919	01/30/1930– 02/16/1931	02/15/1942– 02/04/1943
02/03/1954– 01/23/1955	01/21/1966– 02/08/1967	02/07/1978– 01/27/1979
01/27/1990– 02/14/1991	02/12/2002– 01/31/2003	01/31/2014– 02/18/2015

Goat (aka Ram or Sheep): Positive: appealing, altruistic, creative, empathetic, intuitive, generous, artless, gentle, romantic, sensitive, compliant, candid, and self-effacing darlings. Negative: self-pitying, pessimistic, fugitive, parasitic, vengeful, lazy, indecisive, contentious, violent, capricious, irresponsible, tardy, careless, bigoted, nasty little pieces of work. Equivalent Western sign is **Cancer**.

Years of the Goat/Ram/Sheep

02/01/1919- 02/19/1920	02/17/1931- 02/05/1932	02/05/1943- 01/24/1944
01/24/1955- 02/11/1956	02/09/1967- 01/29/1968	01/28/1979- 02/15/1980
02/15/1991- 02/03/1992	02/01/2003- 01/21/2004	02/19/2015- 02/07/2016

Monkey: Positive: reasonable, faithful, autonomous, candid, altruistic, successful, inventive, co-operative, loving, intelligent, individualistic, and generous entertainers. Negative: hyperemotional, capricious, guileful, self-indulgent, immature, insecure, indifferent, careless, gullible, petty, and grabby scene-stealers. Equivalent Western sign is **Leo**.

Years of the Monkey

02/20/1920- 02/07/1921	02/06/1932- 01/25/1933	01/25/1944- 02/12/1945
02/12/1956- 01/30/1957	01/30/1968- 02/16/1969	02/16/1980- 02/04/1981
02/04/1992- 01/22/1993	01/22/2004- 02/08/2005	02/08/2016- 01/27/2017

Rooster: Positive: forthright, brave, enthusiastic, loyal, hardworking, tenacious, resilient, adventurous, meticulous, prompt, astute, well-dressed, proficient, down-to-earth, gregarious, communicative, sensible, generous, charming, ebullient, and terminally witty. Negative: cranky, fussy, vain, self-involved, blindly egotistical, overzealous, pretentious, materialistic, grabby, high-handed, cynical, mercurial, self-absorbed, and quixotic as hell. Equivalent Western sign is **Virgo**.

Years of the Rooster

02/08/1921- 01/27/1922	01/26/1933- 02/13/1934	02/13/1945- 02/01/1946
01/31/1957- 02/17/1958	02/17/1969- 02/05/1970	02/05/1981- 01/24/1982
01/23/1993- 02/09/1994	02/09/2005- 01/28/2006	01/28/2017- 02/15/2018

Dog: Positive: attentive, well meaning, helpful, warm-hearted, altruistic, modest, devoted, philosophical, dutiful, discreet, intelligent, and enthusiastic. Negative: nasty, mean-spirited, disagreeable, bad-tempered, self-righteous, judgmental, quarrelsome, accusing, nervous, anxious, and impossible to live with. Equivalent Western sign is **Libra**.

Years of the Dog

01/28/1922- 02/15/1923	02/14/1934- 02/03/1935	02/02/1946- 01/21/1947
02/18/1958- 02/07/1959	02/06/1970- 01/26/1971	01/25/1982- 02/12/1983
02/10/1994- 01/30/1995	01/29/2006- 02/17/2007	02/16/2018- 02/04/2019

Pig: Positive: sensible, sensual, sensitive, sweetly naive, caring, self-sacrificing, erudite, talented, open-handed, candid, outgoing, amusing, charitable, obliging, graciously hospitable, and virtuous. Negative: hot-tempered, pessimistic, outrageously epicurean, earthy to a fault, sardonic, snobbish, snide, authoritarian, competitive, know-it-all, stingy, victimized, and sometimes downright criminally mad at the world. Equivalent Western sign is **Scorpio**.

Years of the Pig

02/16/1923- 02/04/1924	02/04/1935- 01/23/1936	01/22/1947- 02/09/1948
02/08/1959- 01/27/1960	01/27/1971- 02/24/1972	02/13/1983- 02/01/1984
01/31/1995- 02/18/1996	02/18/2007- 02/06/2008	02/05/2019- 01/24/2020

Remember:

In addition, Chinese astrology is important in terms of compatibility The grid that follows is taken from http://www.travelchinaguide.com/intro/social_customs/zodiac/ compatibility.htm/. So think of someone you know that may fall under a certain Sun sign and also a certain Chinese Sun sign. Perhaps it explains why some people have such strong SUN signs while others are mixed. It's the combination of these essential ingredients that I think can really explain a person's personality. You decide! Next, we discuss Love Languages, another important ingredient.

Chinese Zodiac Compatibility Grid

Sign	Best Match	Match	No Match
Rat	Dragon, Monkey, Ox	Rat, Tiger, Snake, Dog, Pig	Goat, Horse, Rabbit, Rooster
Ox	Rat, Snake, Rooster	Ox, Tiger, Monkey, Pig	Dragon, Horse, Goat, Dog, Rabbit
Tiger	Horse, Dog	Rat, Ox, Tiger, Rabbit, Dragon, Goat, Rooster, Pig	Snake, Monkey
Rabbit	Goat, Dog, Pig	Tiger, Rabbit, Snake, Monkey	Rat, Ox, Dragon, Rooster, Horse
Dragon	Rat, Monkey, Rooster	Tiger, Snake, Horse, Goat, Pig	Dog, Ox, Dragon, Rabbit
Snake	Ox, Rooster	Rat, Rabbit, Dragon, Snake, Horse, Goat, Dog	Tiger, Monkey, Pig
Horse	Tiger, Goat, Dog	Dragon, Snake, Monkey, Rooster, Pig	Rat, Ox, Rabbit, Horse
Goat	Rabbit, Horse, Pig	Tiger, Dragon, Snake, Goat, Monkey, Rooster	Rat, Ox, Dog
Monkey	Rat, Dragon	Ox, Rabbit, Horse, Goat, Monkey, Rooster, Dog	Tiger, Snake, Pig
Rooster	Ox, Dragon, Snake	Rat, Tiger, Horse, Goat, Monkey, Pig	Rabbit, Rooster, Dog
Dog	Tiger, Rabbit, Horse	Rat, Snake, Monkey, Dog, Pig	Ox, Dragon, Goat, Rooster
Pig	Goat, Rabbit	Rat, Ox, Tiger, Dragon, Horse, Rooster, Dog	Snake, Pig, Monkey

3/4 Cup Love Language

I think it's time to compile some information on Gary Chapman's Five Love Languages. As I've spent time researching the zodiacs, it seemed apparent that a lot of what astrology and birth dates were referring to as temperament and relationship needs were often similar to Chapman's Love Languages, at least in relationship needs. So I researched his five styles and am including them as important ingredients for understanding yourself and your relationships.

Your emotional love language and that of your partner/spouse (or other relationships) may be as different as Mandarin is from

English—no matter how hard you try to say that you love that person in English, if your spouse only understands Mandarin, your words will never mean a thing. We tend to speak our primary love language and become confused when the person we are in a relationship with doesn't understand what we're communicating. Once you identify and learn to speak your partner's primary love language or zodiac, you'll have discovered the key to a long-lasting, loving relationship. Either take the assessment here to discover your own love language(s) (http://www.5lovelanguages.com/profile/) or read more from Dr. Chapman's book: The 5 Love Languages.

Words of Affirmation

This language uses words to affirm other people. So if you like compliments, perhaps this is your love language. Hearing the words "I love you" is important—hearing the reasons behind that love sends your spirits skyward. However, insults can leave you shattered and are not easily forgotten. Thus, for these people, verbal compliments or words of appreciation are powerful communicators of love. So if this is your or your partner's love language, set a goal to give your partner a different compliment each day for a month and make sure to tell your partner how important it is for you to hear the same.

Quality Time

Nothing says "I love you" like full, undivided attention. Being there for this type of person is critical, really being there—with the TV off—makes these people feel truly special and loved. Distractions, postponed dates, or the failure to listen can be especially hurtful. This means giving someone your undivided attention. Some ideas include taking a walk (just the two of you) or going out to eat and looking at each other while talking. But one of the most common is sharing quality conversation—two individuals sharing their thoughts and feelings. If this is your or your partner's love language, ask your partner for a list of activities that he/she'd enjoy doing with you. Then make plans to do one of these once a week or take turns—your favorite activity with your spouse one week and vice versa the next week. Make this a priority in your lives.

Gifts

Don't mistake this love language for materialism. In this case the receiver of gifts thrives on the love, thoughtfulness, and effort behind the gift. If you speak this language, the perfect gift or gesture shows that you are known and cared for. A missed birthday, anniversary, or a hasty, thoughtless gift would be disastrous—so would the absence of everyday gestures. A gift is something you can hold in your hand and say, "Look, my partner was thinking of me," or "My partner remembered me." A gift is a symbol of that thought. Gifts come in all sizes, colors and shapes—some are expensive and others are free. To the individual whose primary love language is receiving gifts, the cost will matter little. If this is your or your partner's love language, both of you should keep a "gift idea" notebook. Every time one of you says, "I really like that," write it down. Select gifts you feel comfortable purchasing, making or finding, and don't wait for a special occasion. Becoming a proficient gift giver is an easy language to learn.

Acts of Service

Can vacuuming the floors really be an expression of love? Absolutely! Anything you do to ease the burden of responsibilities weighing on an "Acts of Service" person will speak volumes. The words he/she most want to hear are "Let me do that for you." Laziness, broken commitments, and making more work for them tell speakers of this language their feelings don't matter. People who speak this love language seek to please their partners by serving them and to express their love for them by doing things for them. Actions, such as cooking a meal, setting a table, washing the dishes, sorting the bills, walking the dog are all acts of service. They require thought, planning, time, effort and energy. If done with a positive spirit, they are indeed expressions of love. If this is your or your partner's love language, ask him/her which acts of service are important to him or her. If both of you value acts of service, compose lists for one another. Another approach would be to notice when you see your partner is stressed and ask what you can do to help.

Physical Touch

Not surprisingly, a person whose primary language is Physical Touch is very touchy. Hugs, pats on the back, holding hands, and thoughtful touches on the arm, shoulder, or face are some of the many ways this individual shows excitement, concern, care, and love. Physical presence and accessibility are crucial while neglect or abuse can be unforgivable and destructive. Holding hands, kissing, hugging and sex—all of these are lifelines for the person for whom physical touch is the primary love language. With it, they feel secure in their partner's love. Touching each other when leaving the house may involve only a brief kiss but speaks volumes. If this is your or your partner's love language, then cuddle or hold hands while sitting together.

Remember:

In summary, your and your partner's love language can tell you a lot about what is needed in your relationship to make it work. Love language is another crucial ingredient in successful relationships.

RANDOM ZODIAC TRIVIA

Lil Wayne, so hey, what's your sign?

Birth date: September 27, 1982

Occupation: American Rapper

Sun Sign: Libra

Chinese Sign: Dog

Lil Wayne (real name: Dwayne Michael Carter, Jr.) makes several references to astrology/zodiacs in his lyrics. Lil Wayne is considered to be one of the top ten rappers of today. Interestingly, we find a lot of Librans in the music industry, including Snoop Dog, Bruno Mars, Ray Charles, Will Smith, Bruce Springsteen, and Usher (and so many others).

Examples of his lyrics:

What's yo name whats yo sign, Zodiac Killer

I'm a Libra and my sign is a scale

So on my Libra scale, I'm weighing sins and forgiveness

Chapter 4: Other Important Ingredients

Strong like cognac what your zodiac; See me I be a Libra and I do everything

Yes I'm nasty as a Scorpio; But I'm a lucky Libra

Um, well it's the Libra baby now come play in my jungle

Chapter 5
Recipes of Hollywood Couples

What I have found over the past year was that it was easy to assess birthdays of those in the public eye, especially celebrities and politicians. There's an abundance of news out there on celebrities, and it was so easy for me to test my recipe compatibility theory using their zodiacs and whether they were compatible with those they were dating at the time. Now granted I only could look up their birthdays, which we now know is only a small ingredient of the full recipe, and it isn't very likely that you can find a celebrity's birth time on Wikipedia! Unfortunately even the MOON sign could be wrong. Again, it's difficult to ascertain a birth chart unless you ask the individuals both their birthday and time—and not everyone knows the time. So below I've gone through a bunch of celebrities' birthdays, but without the time, they could be misleading. I did my best with the power of the internet, looking up birthdays and locations of their birth.

First, let's start with one of the most famous families on television, the Kardashians.

- Kourtney's birthday is April 18, 1979 (ARIES/TAURUS cusp, CAPRICORN moon), and she is dating Scott Disick (born May 26, 1983, GEMINI, SAGITTARIUS moon). They have an interesting relationship: still have not married and do not seem at all compatible on paper. His GEMINI nature explains a lot— talks a lot and loves attention. His combo is compatible with Kourtney's ARIES personality but not the Capricorn moon's more serious side. I can see why she goes back and forth—she has a fun side (Aries) vs. the more serious/practical side (Capricorn).

- Khloe's birthday is June 27, 1984 (CANCER, GEMINI moon). She was married but is now divorcing Lamar Odom (born November 6, 1979, SCORPIO, GEMINI moon). One thing to note about this combination is that it's been said to be the most "like a soul mate," and this couple was very passionate and intense about one another. Hence, the quickie marriage! I used to love watching these two because they empowered all the qualities of a CANCER-SCORPIO relationship (and perhaps even similar emotions/MOON).

- Kim's birthday is October 21, 1980 (LIBRA, PISCES moon). She was married to Kris Humphries (born February 6, 1985, AQUARIUS, VIRGO moon) awhile back. They were very compatible. Perhaps insensitivity was what broke them; their marriage only lasted seventy-four days.

- Kim is now married to Kanye West (born June 8, 1977, GEMINI, PISCES moon), who is definitely a more compatible match (Moon signs are identical; both are sensitive). I think this will work more for Kim, who now has a more compatible mate in multiple ways. An ideal couple, prosperous, happy, good intellectual understanding, great confidence in each other, a successful family life. However, there are always negative aspects in every couple, and there's includes: 1) there are likely to be frequent disputes, as they may find it difficult to speak calmly; 2) they might too frequently adopt an aggressive, defensive, or offensive stance with one another. Conflict could arise if they both want to dominate the other and/or if they do not consciously attempt to relate on the basis of mutual understanding. One (aka Kanye) may lay down the law, give orders, and make decisions; the other may be an independent type (aka Kim) who cannot stand being limited and/or taking orders. They frequently may be impatient with one another, and if they insist on living together, there will be disputes and frequent tension.

Now let's discuss another reality show that took over the U.S. a few years ago, and yes, it was definitely one of my guilty pleasures—aka, The Jersey Shore. Take a look at the birthdays of the cast:

- Snooki—November 23, 1987 (SCORPIO/SAGITTARIUS Cusp, CAPRICORN moon)

- JWOWW—February 27, 1986 (PISCES, LIBRA moon)

- Vinny—November 11, 1987 (SCORPRIO, CANCER moon)

- Sammi—March 14, 1987 (PISCES, VIRGO moon)

- Ronnie—December 4, 1985 (SAGITTARIUS, VIRGO moon)

- Pauly—July 5, 1980 (CANCER, ARIES moon)

- Mike—July 4, 1982 (CANCER, SAGITTARIUS moon)

- Deena—January 12, 1987 (CAPRICORN, GEMINI moon)

- Jionni—March 20, 1987 (PISCES, SAGITTARIUS moon)—very compatible with Snooki!

- Roger—June 1, 1975 (GEMINI, PISCES moon)—very compatible with JWOWW!

Notice anything interesting about these birthdays? Well, one thing that stuck out to me right away was that the majority of their birthdays were PISCES, CANCER, and SCORPIO, all WATER signs, driven by emotion and a hell-of-a-lot more likely to be DRAMA QUEENS! Thus, it should be no surprise to anyone that these individuals thrive on drama and emotional outbursts. They are moody and irritable and sensitive. I was also interested in the dynamic between Ronnie (SAGITTARIUS) and Sammi (PISCES), which isn't very compatible—Sammi is probably too sensitive and emotional for the fiery Ronnie. However, looking at their MOON signs (without the time of birth, it is less reliable), I found that they both had VIRGO moons, which explains perhaps why they are so compatible. They still have quite a lot of issues, but I can see why they work.

So let's spend some time examining some famous celebrity couples! I'll try to explain the compatibilities of the fifty hottest celebrity couples today.

Angelina Jolie & Brad Pitt

Brad Pitt (born December 18, 1963; Shawnee, OK; SAGITTARIUS; CAPRICORN moon) is married to Angelina Jolie (born June 4, 1975; Los Angeles, CA; GEMINI; ARIES moon). These two are compatible in sun signs. A favorable union, a joyful family life. However, this combo (GEMINI + SAG) is often called the heaven and hell compatibility. They are somewhat compatible but could definitely have some heated arguments due to his Capricorn and her Aries emotions. I think the hell part will come eventually for this couple. They don't always share the same ideas, their tastes are different and this leads to a few tense moments due to lack of understanding.

Jennifer Aniston & Justin Paul Theroux

Brad Pitt was first married to Jennifer Aniston (born February 11, 1969; Sherman Oaks, CA; AQUARIUS; SAGITTARIUS moon), which was somewhat compatible. She is now with Justin Paul Theroux (born August 10, 1971; Washington, D.C.; LEO; ARIES moon). Even though LEOS and AQUARIANS are opposites, they still work, and Jennifer and Justin's MOON signs (emotions) are very much in line so this should work. On paper Justin seems to be a better match for Jennifer. They boost each other's confidence and fill each other with enthusiasm. Here is a couple you can call stable. They will lead their life together quietly with friendship slowly replacing love.

Beyonce & Jay-Z

Beyonce (born September 4, 1981; Houston, TX; VIRGO; SCORPIO Moon) married Jay-Z (born December 4, 1969; Brooklyn, NY; SAGITTARIUS; LIBRA moon), and they are not very compatible, not at all! Beyonce is ruled more by Earth and Water so relationships can be extremely passionate and somewhat possessive while Jay-Z is ruled by his rational side (Fire and Air), which may place strain on their relationship eventually, due to their incompatible Sun and Moon signs; however, other important ingredients are missing (i.e., ascendant, planets) which could explain their relationship better. Misunderstandings may be frequent, and they are draining. If at first the relationship is charming and agreeable, it will quickly become disharmonious, and life together will become unbearable. If one of the two does not make an effort or does not find a compromise, it will lead irrevocably to a breakup. However, they are charming, agreeable and know how to entertain their friends generously and warmly. They go well together and love each other in a discrete and sincere way. They appreciate the joys of life together, and both have a good spiritual understanding. Both parties must be committed to happiness in order for this to work. This is a union that is particularly based on physical understanding and passionate love. There is a lot of affection between them, and they need to express it physically.

Victoria Beckham & David Beckham

Victoria (born April 17, 1974; Essex, England; ARIES; AQUARIUS moon) and David Beckham (born May 2, 1975; London, England; TAURUS; AQUARIUS moon) are compatible emotionally, but probably have a passionate and conflicted relationship. I'm guessing they butt heads a lot, both being very stubborn. But with their similar moons, they're compatible and quite unique. An ideal couple, prosperous, happy, good intellectual understanding, great confidence in each other, a successful family life. The attraction is certainly there, but the relationship can lose its innocence quite easily. This is a union that is particularly based on physical understanding, passionate love. There is a lot of affection between them, and they need to express it physically. At the beginning, they will appreciate each other a lot, and will have pleasure in being together but, quite quickly, this life will become unbearable with disputes, conflicts and crying replacing love.

Gisele Bundchen & Tom Brady

Gisele (born July 20, 1980; Rio Grande do Sul, Brazil; CANCER/ LEO cusp; SCORPIO Moon) and Tom (born August 3, 1977; San Mateo, CA; LEO; ARIES Moon) have the Leo personalities but very different and incompatible moon signs, which could be problematic, since their moons just seem to clash. They have good intentions towards each other, but they often promise more than they can deliver. They make big plans that often fail to be realized. When one person wants to spend "together time," the other feels restless and dreams of being somewhere else. Freedom versus closeness is a conflict that arises often in this relationship. There can be a certain level of self-consciousness together that is always present, no matter how long they are together. There is a lot of loyalty between them, and a feeling of responsibility for one another.

Faith Hill & Tim McGraw:

Faith (born September 21, 1967; Ridgeland, MS; VIRGO/LIBRA cusp; TAURUS moon) and Tim (born May 1, 1967; Delhi, LA; TAURUS; AQUARIUS moon) are very compatible because of her TAURUS moon, and LIBRA cusp. Her "cusp" helps with the Earth and AIR combos. A life together with few problems. Love tends to develop into friendship. In a broad sense, they understand each other and go well together. Their relationship can be a little routine at times, and there may be some self-consciousness with each other. This is one indication that they will be faithful to one another. They stimulate each other to be more creative and expressive. They learn a great deal from each other. They understand each other, like to discuss things with each other and undertake joint initiatives. Great intellectual understanding. Jealousy, possessiveness, and resentment are very possible. If the relationship ends, it is difficult to remain friends, as one person feels burned. They sometimes encourage impracticality in one another. They often feel let down with one another, usually because each wants very much to please the other, but it is hard to fulfill all the promises that are made to one another.

Jada Pinkett Smith & Will Smith

Jada (born September 18, 1971; Baltimore, MD; VIRGO/LIBRA cusp; VIRGO moon) and Will (born September 25, 1968; West Philadelphia, PA; LIBRA; SCORPIO Moon) are quite compatible, the LIBRA is present for both and they can view each other's arguments with ease. Will is much more passionate emotionally than the cool-natured Jada. It's not only about love, it's about "like." They go well together, they love each other, and feel good, happy and radiant in each other's company. There is much attraction. They are capable of charming each other. Sometimes, they gloss over problems and conflicts just in order to keep the peace, which is not a good idea in the long run. Union or love will be very strong, not at all intellectual, but sensual and full of romanticism and originality. It's love-at-first-sight, the great passion: they will be drawn to each other like two magnets, they will always have to see and touch each other. Very good sexual understanding, typically very passionate. It must be said that this type of relationship may not last forever, it may not develop into a quiet and tender love. If they part, it is close to impossible to stay friends because of the constant reminder of the passion that once existed. It's all or nothing with them. However, if they stay together, there is strength to gain from each other. Tolerance exists between them.

Jessica Biel & Justin Timberlake

Jessica (born March 3, 1982; Ely, MN; PISCES; GEMINI moon) is married to Justin (born January 31, 1981; Memphis, TN; AQUARIUS; SAGITTARIUS moon) and these two are mostly compatible. She's probably much more emotional and sensitive than Justin, who may be more likely to value his freedom. However, her AIR moon helps with his AIR and FIRE behaviors. They are able to solve problems when they put their heads together. Respect for each other's intelligence. Good understanding between them and intellectual interests in common. A life together with few problems. Love tends to develop into friendship. In a broad sense, they understand each other and go well together. Their relationship can be a little routine at times, and there may be some self-consciousness with each other. This is one indication that they will be faithful to one another. A very strong but destructive, passion to be avoided if at all possible. Jealousy, possessiveness, and resentment are very possible. If the relationship ends, it is difficult to remain friends, as one person feels burned.

Gwyneth Paltrow & Chris Martin

Gwyneth (born September 27, 1972; Los Angeles, CA; LIBRA; GEMINI moon) and Chris (born March 2, 1977; Devon, England; PISCES; LEO moon) do not seem compatible – she's ruled by her rational side and he is probably more sensitive and emotionally driven, which helps with his music. But I'm not sure how it helps with their relationship (no one will believe me but I wrote this 2 years before they announced their recent separation!). This relationship can only bring illusions, and therefore also disappointments will follow. These two people can never understand each other and if they insist on living together, it will be with lies and deception. There can be a certain level of self-consciousness together that is always present, no matter how long they are together. There is a lot of loyalty between them, and a feeling of responsibility for one another. The attraction is strong, but there is something inconstant in this partnership. It may be that the feelings run hot and cold, or that circumstances are such that their romantic feelings for one another are interrupted often.

Jennifer Garner & Ben Affleck

Jennifer (born April 17, 1972; Houston, TX; ARIES; GEMINI moon) and Ben (born August 15, 1972; Berkeley, CA; LEO; SCORPIO moon) have excellent personality compatibilities but am a little concerned about their emotions that conflict (AIR and WATER). Here is a couple you like to be with. They are charming, agreeable and know how to entertain their friends generously and warmly. They go well together, and love each other in a discrete and sincere way, and appreciate the joys of life together. A life together that can be very challenging at times on an intellectual level. Intellectual misunderstandings, diametrically opposed tastes, different ideas.

Love tends to develop into friendship. In a broad sense, they understand each other and go well together. Their relationship can be a little routine at times, and there may be some self-consciousness with each other.

Nicole Kidman & Keith Urban

Nicole (born June 20, 1967; Honolulu, HI; GEMINI/CANCER cusp; SAGITTARIUS moon) and Keith (born October 26, 1967; Northland, New Zealand; SCORPIO; CANCER moon) are not very compatible, but Nicole's CANCER cusp helps since they are ruled by their emotions. Keith may be at times too sensitive for her take-charge moon sign. (Note: Tom Cruise was a Cancer.) Their relationship will sometimes be agreeable, sometimes disturbed. They will like to share their ideas which are not always to the other's taste, so that they may have interminable discussions in order to convince each other of their mistakes, lack of judgment or lack of taste. At the beginning, they will appreciate each other a lot, and will have pleasure in being together, but quite quickly, this life will become unbearable with disputes, conflicts and crying replacing love.

Katie Holmes & Tom Cruise

Katie (born December 18, 1978; Toledo, OH; SAGITTARIUS; LEO Moon) and Tom (born July 3, 1962; Syracuse, NY; CANCER; LEO moon) are not very compatible and may explain a reason for their divorce. Tom is probably way too emotional (hence CANCER) and moody for Katie's more rational side. However, both had LEO moons, meaning they both wanted to be the center of attention in their relationships, which they might have competed with one another for this. However, the LEO moons explain why they were connected instantly to one another and lasted as long as they did. His CANCER side is probably what attracted Nicole Kidman for awhile, since she is on the cusp. The attraction is strong, but there is something inconstant in this partnership. It may be that the feelings run hot and cold, or that circumstances are such that their romantic feelings for one another are interrupted often. A tendency to want to direct the partner's thoughts and ideas. Reading too much into what is said and what is not said. This relationship can only bring illusions, and therefore also disappointments will follow. These two people can never understand each other and if they insist on living together, it will be with lies and deception. They often feel let down with one another, usually because each wants very much to please the other, but it is hard to fulfill all the promises that are made to one another.

Fergie & Josh Duhamel

Fergie (born March 27, 1975; Hacienda Heights, CA; ARIES; LIBRA Moon) and Josh (born November 14, 1972; Minot, ND; SCORPIO; AQUARIUS moon) are compatible only because of Josh's AQUARIUS moon, which is great with Fergie's playful ARIES and LIBRA signs (FIRE and AIR). This is a union that is particularly based on physical understanding and passionate love. There is a lot of affection between them, and they need to express it physically. Plenty of attraction here. There is a level of forgiveness and mercy in the chemistry between them. They may share dreams together with a sense of freedom. Tolerance exists between the two of them.

Kelly Ripa & Mark Consuelos

Kelly (born October 2, 1970; Stratford, NJ; LIBRA; SCORPIO Moon) and Mark (born March 30, 1971; Zaragoza, Spain; ARIES; TAURUS moon) are quite compatible especially with their sun personalities. Their moon signs match up somewhat, Kelly being a lot more passionate, while Mark is a lot more traditional, but both need and require stability. Interestingly, his moon will prevent him from ever breaking apart, so she'll have to do it, if they ever do. Here is a couple that may have frequent disputes, as they may find it difficult to speak calmly. They might too frequently adopt an aggressive, defensive, or offensive stance with one another. Conflict is caused if they both want to dominate the other, and if they do not consciously attempt to relate on the basis of mutual understanding. One may lay down the law, give orders, and make decisions and the other may be an independent type, who cannot stand being limited or taking orders. They make each other impatient and easily frustrate each other. The sexual attraction is unique and powerful at first, seeming to arise suddenly and unexpectedly. However, it is a temperamental attraction and can leave just as suddenly. The attraction is certainly there, but the relationship can lose its innocence quite easily. Positive aspect: A life together with few problems. Love tends to develop into friendship. In a broad sense, they understand each other and go well together. Their relationship can be a little routine at times, and there may be some self-consciousness with each other.

Sarah Jessica Parker & Matthew Broderick

Sarah (born March 25, 1965; Nelsonville, OH; ARIES; CAPRICORN Moon) and Matthew (born March 21, 1962; New York, NY; PISCES/ARIES cusp; LIBRA moon) are mostly compatible and fulfill each other personality wise and emotionally somewhat (she's probably more reserved emotionally, but he prefers being in a relationship), which probably explains why they've been married so long. A life together with few problems. Love tends to develop into friendship. In a broad sense, they understand each other and go well together. Their relationship can be a little routine at times, and there may be some self-consciousness with each other. They can interrupt each other often. Problems can arise when one or the other finds their partner too blunt or too critical. When involved in a conversation, they can compete for the microphone. Conversations can be very lively, but may often escalate into arguments.

Megan Fox & Brian Austin Green

Megan (born May 16, 1986; Oak Ridge, TN; TAURUS; LEO moon) and Brian (born July 15, 1973; Van Nuys, CA; CANCER; CAPRICORN moon) are compatible due to their similar EARTH signs, both are very grounded and practical. Brian is probably a little more needy and emotional than Megan due to his Cancer personality, but with his moon, that keeps emotions in check. I can't be sure, perhaps he's a little more up and down in emotions. They make each other impatient and easily frustrated. The sexual attraction is unique and powerful at first, seeming to arise suddenly and unexpectedly. However, it is a temperamental attraction and can leave just as suddenly. Conflict is caused if they both want to dominate the other, and if they do not consciously attempt to relate on the basis of mutual understanding. One may lay down the law, give orders, and make decisions and the other may be an independent type, who cannot stand being limited or taking orders. Positive aspect: This union could be favorable and lasting if they are really looking for a mature person to be with. There can be a certain level of self-consciousness together that is always present, no matter how long they are together. There is a lot of loyalty between them, and a feeling of responsibility for one another.

Coco & Ice-T

Coco (born March 17, 1979; Palos Verdes, CA; PISCES; SCORPIO moon) and Ice (born February 16, 1958; Newark, NJ; AQUARIUS/PISCES cusp; AQUARIUS moon) are not at all compatible, and the only hope for them is Ice's cusp which places him in a more emotional/sensitive WATER compatibility. But Ice probably values freedom and rationality a lot more than the passionate and emotion-driven Coco. A relationship which will be agreeable, they will like to speak to each other, have a good intellectual understanding, their tastes will be very similar, they will like to share their feelings with each other. They can interrupt each other often. Problems can arise when one or the other finds their partner too blunt or too critical. When involved in a conversation, they can compete for the microphone. Conversations can be very lively, but may often escalate into arguments. A life together with few problems. Love tends to develop into friendship. In a broad sense, they understand each other and go well together. Their relationship can be a little routine at times, and there may be some self-consciousness with each other. A life together that can be very challenging at times on an intellectual level.

Kendra Wilkinson & Hank Baskett

Kendra (born June 12, 1985; San Diego, CA; GEMINI; ARIES moon) and Hank (born September 4, 1982; Clovis, NM; VIRGO; PISCES moon) are not compatible; she's ruled by her AIR and FIRE signs, uses her rational side in situations, whereas Hank is EARTH and WATER and is probably more grounded and sensitive. I don't see this lasting very long, unless their Ascendant signs are more in alignment. They have good intentions towards each other, but they often promise more than they can deliver. They make big plans that often fail to be realized. When one person wants to spend "together time," the other feels restless and dreams of being somewhere else. Freedom versus closeness is a conflict that arises often in this relationship. It's love-at-first-sight, the great passion: they will be drawn to each other like two magnets, they will always have to see and touch each other. Very good sexual understanding, typically very passionate. It must be said that this type of relationship may not last forever. If they part, one will suffer when the passion of the other dies, it will be a very difficult time to live through. However, if they stay together, there is strength to gain from each other.

Tori Spelling & Dean McDermott

Tori (born May 16, 1973; Los Angeles, CA; TAURUS; SCORPIO moon) and Dean (born November 16, 1966; Ontario, Canada; SCORPIO; CAPRICORN moon) are fairly compatible. They may not match up completely with their SUN and MOONS, but they match up cross-wise. They can fulfill each other's needs, but just have to adjust. Lack of understanding between the two persons can frequently cause disruptions. They may not have the same intellectual interests or the same tastes and this can result in problems understanding each other or feeling as if they are on the same page. This could lead to conflicts, lies, etc. It is very challenging for such a union to be happy, but if it progresses, it could easily become unbearable! Both parties must be committed to happiness in order for this to work. The two persons are drawn towards each other, but the union is unstable, because there will inevitably be division, probably through misunderstanding on the sexual level, which may frustrate the partner. Positive aspect: This union is likely to be completely successful. A couple that is happy to be alive, and to live together, with a pleasant family and home, total confidence in each other, intellectual understanding, similar tastes. There is a strong desire to make each other happy. They enjoy each other's company immensely and put each other in a happy mood. Forgiveness and graciousness characterizes this partnership.

Bethenny Frankel & Jason Hoppy

Bethenny (born November 4, 1970; New York, NY; SCORPIO; CAPRICORN moon) and Jason (born September 4, 1970; New York, NY; VIRGO; LIBRA moon) are somewhat compatible because they have EARTH elements present. Bethenny is the essential SCORPIO/CAPRICORN combo I think – she's so passionate about everything that she does and one of the hardest workers. However, these two are now divorced. It's too easy for this relationship to end up becoming manipulative and frustrating. A difficult union that can succeed, but could involve some distancing and dishonesty. Deceptions have a way of coming to the light and great disappointments are possible as a result. Favorable union of the minds. They speak to each other about things they never talk about to others.

Eva Mendes & Ryan Gosling

Eva (born March 5, 1974; Miami, FL; PISCES; LEO moon) is dating Ryan (born November 12, 1980; Ontario, Canada; SCORPIO; CAPRICORN moon) and I see this lasting for awhile, since both are WATER signs. Ryan at one time dated Rachel McAdams (born November 17, 1978; Ontario, Canada; SCORPIO; GEMINI moon), who seemed like a good fit, both SCORPIOs, but perhaps their Moon signs were not compatible enough; Rachel being too flirty and fun for the more serious Ryan. However, Eva's dominating LEO moon may also be too much for Ryan's more serious CAPRICORN moon. Their relationship will sometimes be agreeable, sometimes disturbed. They will like to share their ideas which are not always to the other's taste, so that they may have interminable discussions in order to convince each other of their mistakes, lack of judgment or lack of taste. They boost each other's confidence and fill each other with enthusiasm. They make plans together, and they are realistic enough to fulfill. They frequently are impatient with each other. If they insist on living together, there will be disputes and frequent tension.

Camila Alves & Matthew McConaughey

Camila (born May 27, 1982; Minas Gerais, Brazil; GEMINI; LEO moon) is married to Matthew (born November 4, 1969; Uvalde, TX; SCORPIO; VIRGO moon) and these two do not seem compatible on paper, perhaps their Ascendant signs or VENUS love styles are compatible. Camila is more ruled by her AIR and FIRE side, whereas Matthew is passionately ruled by his WATER and EARTH elements. An ideal couple, prosperous, happy, good intellectual understanding, great confidence in each other, a successful family life. Great passionate affair, very intense and transforming. They feel that the relationship forces them to grow. A life together in which each will desire the other and satisfy each other's sexual needs. Frustration levels tend to be minimal, and this helps the couple develop a pleasant atmosphere between them. They may do great things together or simply inspire one another. Their styles in expressing love, and their preferred way to receive love, are at odds. This can be a real nuisance because there can be a lot of misunderstandings and wasted energy trying to explain oneself.

Rita Wilson & Tom Hanks

Rita was born October 26, 1956; Los Angeles, CA (SCORPIO; LEO moon) and Tom was born July 9, 1956; Concord, CA (CANCER, LEO moon) – you couldn't be MORE compatible! These two have the "soul mate" type of SCORPIO-CANCER compatibility and identical emotional MOONs to be happy. They are able to solve problems when they put their heads together. Respect for each other's intelligence. Good understanding between the two persons and intellectual interests in common. Similar or harmonious type of curiosity. They respect each other's goals and drives, and don't stand in the way of their attempts to achieve their goals. Their body rhythms match well, and they share a basic physical bond that is hard to break. Energizing. A life together in which each will desire the other and satisfy each other's sexual needs. Frustration levels tend to be minimal, and this helps the couple develop a pleasant atmosphere between them. They may do great things together or simply inspire one another.

Mariah Carey & Nick Cannon

Mariah was born March 27, 1970; Huntington, NY (ARIES; SAGITTARIUS moon) and Nick was born October 8, 1980; San Diego, CA (LIBRA; LIBRA moon). There is definitely good compatibility between these two, but Nick is probably always the one accommodating Mariah's feisty temper and passionate emotions. Enormous physical passion. The sexual attraction is intense and insistent. They want to be around each other as much as possible. Their sexual relationship evolves with time, instead of dissolves. A very strong passion but destructive, to be avoided if at all possible. Jealousy, possessiveness, and resentment are very possible. If the relationship ends, it is difficult to remain friends, as one person feels burned. This union could be favorable and lasting, if they are really looking for a mature person to be with. There can be a certain level of self-consciousness together that is always present, no matter how long they are together. There is a lot of loyalty between them, and a feeling of responsibility for one another.

Jennifer Lopez & Casper Smart

Jennifer Lopez (born July 24, 1969; The Bronx, NY; LEO; SCORPIO moon) married and divorced Mark Anthony (born September 16,

1968; New York, NY; VIRGO; CANCER moon). Perhaps their emotions were compatible, but their personality/SUN signs were not (imagine continual conflict/fighting). She dated and recently broke up with Beau "Casper" Smart (born April 7, 1987; Anaheim, CA; ARIES/CANCER moon). Pure sexual attraction can unite the couple. They feel as if they have an ideal partner. They will be energetic, full of life and can undertake things together on a professional level or travel together on adventurous, unpredictable journeys. However, his infidelity lead to their breakup. JLo recently stated that Ben Affleck might have been the "one who got away" which makes sense since he is a LEO/SCORPIO combo which is identical to JLo's signs! Those two were spot on. They respect each other's goals and drives, and don't stand in the way of their attempts to achieve their goals. Their body rhythms match well, and they share a basic physical bond that is hard to break. Energizing. They boost each other's confidence and fill each other with enthusiasm. They make plans together, and they are realistic enough to fulfill them. There is a tendency to want to direct the partner's thoughts and ideas. Reading too much into what is said and what is not said.

Catherine Zeta Jones & Michael Douglas

Catherine (born September 25, 1969; Swansea, Wales; LIBRA; PISCES moon) and Michael (born September 25, 1944; New Brunswick, NJ; LIBRA; CAPRICORN moon) are both LIBRAs and born on the same day! Michael's CAPRICORN moon is a great match for Catherine's PISCES moon. Here is a couple that may have frequent disputes, as they may find it difficult to speak calmly. They might too frequently adopt an aggressive, defensive, or offensive stance with one another. Conflict is caused if they both want to dominate the other, and if they do not consciously attempt to relate on the basis of mutual understanding. One may lay down the law, give orders, and make decisions and the other may be an independent type, who cannot stand being limited, taking orders. It's an excellent aspect for a union because neither has to explain to the other about his or her life goals and overall personality. The two people complement each other in basic ways. It's too easy for this relationship to end up becoming manipulative and frustrating. A difficult union that can succeed, but could involve some distancing and dishonesty.

Demi Moore & Ashton Kutcher & Mila Kunis

Demi (born November 11, 1962; Roswell, NM; SCORPIO; TAURUS moon) and Ashton (born February 7, 1978; Cedar Rapids, IA; AQUARIUS; AQUARIUS moon) divorced. These two are VERY incompatible (Scorpio and Aquarius – OUCH!), and even their moons were poorly matched – TAURUS and AQUARIUS – another big OUCH! Demi was probably more relationship-oriented, while Ashton valued his independence and freedom. The two persons are drawn towards each other, but the union is unstable because there will inevitably be division, probably through misunderstanding on the sexual level, which may frustrate the partner. Their styles in expressing love, and their preferred way to receive love, are at odds. This can be a real nuisance because there can be a lot of misunderstandings and wasted energy trying to explain oneself. Demi Moore was formerly married to Bruce Willis (born March 19, 1955; Idar-Oberstein, Germany; PISCES/ARIES cusper; CAPRICORN moon), and him being a PISCES was much more compatible with her (as well as their Earth moons). The ARIES feisty nature was probably too much for their relationship due to her TAURUS moon, however. Ashton and Mila (DOB: August 14, 1983; Chernivtsi, Ukraine; LEO; SCORPIO moon) are now engaged and are somewhat more matched (his Aquarius and her Leo are technically opposites) and I'm not very confident about her SCORPIO, which is another version of Demi's relationship. Perhaps they have other compatible elements that I am not able to see (planets, ascendant, etc). This aspect shows an attraction to each other beyond the physical. There is a level of forgiveness and mercy in the chemistry between them. They share dreams together with a sense of freedom. Tolerance exists between them. A life together in which each will desire the other and satisfy each other's sexual needs. Frustration levels tend to be minimal, and this helps the couple develop a pleasant atmosphere between them. They may do great things together or simply inspire one another.

Ellen DeGeneres & Portia de Rossi

Ellen (DOB: January 26, 1958; Metairie, LA; AQUARIUS; ARIES moon) and Portia (DOB: January 31, 1973; Victoria, Australia; AQUARIUS; CAPRICORN moon) are both Aquarians and are very compatible! For Ellen, social relationships are extremely important to her, she is generally charming with an easy-going manner. Her Aries moon makes her a good leader and child-like; someone who loves to have fun. Based on their (incompatible) moon signs, Ellen is more of the do-er while Portia is the less emotional partner in the relationship with her Capricorn moon (very practical and hardworking). It's not only about love, it's about "like." It would be a good idea to schedule plenty of leisure time together, especially when other problems arise in the relationship, if only to remind each other how much they truly enjoy each other's company, tastes, and interests. They go well together, they love each other, and feel good, happy and radiant in each other's company. There is much attraction. They are capable of charming each other. Sometimes, they gloss over problems and conflicts just in order to keep the peace, which is not a good idea in the long run. A relationship which will be agreeable, they will like to speak to each other, have a good intellectual understanding, their tastes will be very similar, they will like to share their feelings with each other. A life together with few problems. Love tends to develop into friendship. In a broad sense, they understand each other and go well together. Their relationship can be a little routine at times, and there may be some self-consciousness with each other. There is a level of forgiveness and mercy in the chemistry between them.

Jennifer Love Hewitt & Brian Hallisay

Jennifer (DOB: February 21, 1979; Waco, TX; PISCES; SAGITTARIUS) is married to Brian (DOB: October 31, 1978; Washington, D.C.; SCORPIO; SCORPIO). Their emotionally driven compatibility works great, however their emotions are incompatible, so other elements are needed for their union to last. A very strong passion but destructive, to be avoided if at all possible. Jealousy, possessiveness, and resentment are very possible. If the relationship ends, it is difficult to remain friends, as one person feels burned. Complete respect for each other's romantic style. They don't easily offend each other and instinctively understand what makes the other person happy. Conflicts arise, but they are generally smoothed over with ease, as there is good will between them. Very good aspect for a successful union. Love, gaiety, understanding.

Miranda Lambert & Blake Shelton

Miranda (DOB: November 10, 1983; Longview, TX; SCORPIO; CAPRICORN) is married to Blake (DOB: June 18, 1976; Ada, OK; GEMINI; PISCES) and are somewhat compatible due to Blake's

PISCES moon sign, otherwise, their personalities are quite strange together. This explains why Blake talks a lot on the Voice, however! And how he's super compatible with his love, Adam Levine on the show (Adam is a PISCES). It's love-at-first-sight, the great passion: they will be drawn to each other like two magnets, they will always have to see and touch each other. The attraction is certainly there, but the relationship can lose its innocence quite easily. Here is a couple that may have frequent disputes, as they may find it difficult to speak calmly. They might too frequently adopt an aggressive, defensive, or offensive stance with one another. Conflict is caused if they both want to dominate the other, and if they do not consciously attempt to relate on the basis of mutual understanding. One may lay down the law, give orders, and make decisions and the other may be an independent type, who cannot stand being limited, taking orders. A love that is particularly based on physical understanding, a passionate love with all its negative sides: possessiveness, jealousy, aggressiveness. Such a union is unlikely to last, but if it does, there are a lot of hurt feelings and stormy confrontations. The sexual attraction is especially strong at the beginning, but disagreements often have a major impact on the sex life. They end up on opposite ends of the couch frequently. While they get on well when they first meet, sharing the same ideas and tastes, with the years, their ideas change and they do not develop in the same way. They will no longer understand each other and could split up because they no longer love each other or have nothing more in common.

Jessie James & Eric Decker

Jessie (born April 12, 1988; Vicenza, Italy; ARIES, AQUARIUS moon) is married to Eric (born March 15, 1987; Cold Spring, MN; PISCES, VIRGO moon). Looking at these two, I don't see a lot of compatibility as she is ruled by FIRE and AIR, thus rationality and less emotional, while Eric is ruled by WATER and EARTH. Hopefully there are other elements that are compatible in their charts. Difficult relationship as a couple, the two being too different even to complement each other. Here is a couple you can call stable. They will lead their life together quietly, with friendship slowly replacing love. Jessie will dominate Eric - as is only natural - but Eric might find this difficult to accept. In any case, as Eric likes to feel secure, Jessie is a perfect partner. Negative aspect: An unfavorable union, nothing in common. A very strong passion but destructive, to be avoided if at all possible. Jealousy, possessiveness, and resentment are very possible. If the relationship ends, it is difficult to remain friends, as one person feels burned.

Amber Heard & Johnny Depp

Amber (born April 4, 1986; Austin, TX; TAURUS, LIBRA moon) is engaged to Johnny (born June 9, 1963; Owensboro, KY; GEMINI, CAPRICORN moon). He previously dated Vanessa Paradis (born December 22, 1972; Val-de-Marne, France; CAPRICORN, CANCER moon). Amber is a better match of EARTH and AIR for him, without the moody Cancer-side of Vanessa, perhaps. Lack of understanding between the two persons can frequently cause disruptions. They may not have the same intellectual interests or the same tastes and this can result in problems understanding each other or feeling as if they are on the same page. This could lead to conflicts, lies, etc. This is a union that is particularly based on physical understanding, passionate love. There is a lot of affection between them, and they need to express it physically. A life together in which each will desire the other and satisfy each other's sexual needs. Frustration levels tend to be minimal, and this helps the couple develop a pleasant atmosphere between them. They may do great things together or simply inspire one another. There is an ability to bring imagination and fantasy successfully to the relationship.

Prince William & Kate Middleton

Prince William (born June 21, 1982; London, England; GEMINI/CANCER, GEMINI moon) is married to Kate Middleton (born January 9, 1982; Berkshire, England; CAPRICORN, CANCER moon). These two are mostly compatible with William's CANCER-cusp, but their emotions are quite polar opposite. Favorable for all types of communication. It is so easy to get the ideas flowing. Great mental energy between the two. They respect each other's minds. They stimulate each other to be more creative and expressive. They learn a great deal from each other. They understand each other, like to discuss things with each other and undertake joint initiatives. Great intellectual understanding. They may do great things together or simply inspire one another. FYI: Prince Harry was born on September 15, 1984; London, England; VIRGO, TAURUS moon. He's a very EARTHY gentleman, very serious, practical and hardworking. He definitely needs an EARTH or WATER partner.

Prince George of Cambridge (DOB: July 22, 2013; LEO/CANCER cusp; CAPRICORN moon; SCORPIO ascendant) has a lot of CANCER in his birth chart, and since his birth info is so publicized, I found it easy to find out all his information and plugged it in, and am pasting verbatim (I am not making any of this up!): You have a great urge to go farther or deeper into life every step of the way. You want to experience more, and your desires are both powerful and intense. It is hard for you to find satisfaction in common experiences, and you have magnetic power if you choose to use it wisely. You are fascinated with what lies under the surface, and at some point in your life, self-improvement is a big interest. You are attracted to unexplored or taboo areas of life, and you avoid all things superficial. Financial problems may ease after marriage. You want to be considered an accomplished and important person, and when you face obstacles, you don't always see that you are your own worst enemy. You may long to be considered important in the eyes of the world, yet you harbor fear of success at the same time. You take failures and minor setbacks to heart, and may even practically beat yourself up over them. Self-awareness to the point of real self-consciousness is a possibility. The truth is, nobody holds a microscope over you, except for yourself. It is easy and natural for you to be received well by others. There is a distinct air of authority and magnanimity surrounding you. The authority you project generally doesn't offend others, generally because sincerity is sensed at the same time. Most people would describe you as natural, easy to like, and friendly. You may have a marked interest in the performing arts and/or sports and games, both as a spectator and participant. This is an especially favorable aspect to have for those who are in the public eye.

Chrissy Teigen & John Legend

Chrissy (born November 30, 1985; Delta, UT; SAGITTARIUS, CANCER moon) is married to John (born December 28, 1978; Springfield, OH; CAPRICORN, SAGITTARIUS moon). They are a great match, as they have the Sagittarius in both of them, and the EARTH/WATER combos are great together. Here is a couple you like to be with. They are charming, agreeable and know how to entertain their friends generously and warmly. They go well together, and love each other in a discrete and sincere way, and appreciate the joys of life together. Few clouds in this couple's life, at least on an intellectual level. They have a good intellectual understanding, take pleasure in being together and in discussing and exchanging ideas. Together, they can come up with unique and creative ideas and solutions to problems. This aspect shows an attraction to each other beyond the physical. There is a level of forgiveness and mercy in the chemistry. Complete respect for each other's romantic style. They don't easily offend each other and instinctively understand what makes the other person happy. Conflicts arise, but they are generally smoothed over with ease, as there is good will between them. Very good aspect for a successful union. Love, gaiety, understanding. Positive aspect: Enormous physical passion. The sexual attraction is intense and insistent. They want to be around each other as much as possible. Their sexual relationship evolves with time, instead of dissolves.

Giuliana & Bill Rancic

Giuliana (born August 17, 1975; Naples, Italy; LEO, CAPRICORN moon) is married to Bill (born May 16, 1971; Chicago, IL; TAURUS, AQUARIUS moon). At first glance, yikes when you see a LEO/TAURUS match – imagine a lot of butting heads (bull vs. lion). However, they both have EARTH in them to keep them grounded; and LEOS and AQUARIANS go well together. A lot of energy is wasted in having to explain yourselves to each other. Misunderstandings are frequent, and they are draining. If one of the two does not make an effort, or does not find a compromise, it leads irrevocably to a breakup. They frequently are impatient with each other. If they insist on living together, there will be disputes and frequent tension. Positive aspect: This union is likely to be completely successful. A couple that is happy to be alive, and to live together, with a pleasant family and home, total confidence in each other (and with reason), intellectual understanding, similar tastes. There is a strong desire to make each other happy. You enjoy each other's company immensely and you put each other in a happy mood. You make each other laugh and you feel very open, loose, and jovial around each other. Forgiveness and graciousness characterizes your partnership. It would be a good idea to schedule plenty of leisure time together, especially when other problems arise in the relationship, if only to remind each other how much they truly enjoy each other's company, tastes, and interests. They go well together, they love each other, and feel good, happy and radiant in each other's company. There is much attraction, especially on the part of the Venus person. They are capable of charming each other. Sometimes, they gloss over problems and conflicts just in order to keep the peace, which is not a good idea in the long run. They will lead their life together quietly, with friendship slowly replacing love. A meeting that could be passing and highly disappointing in the end. The attraction is strong, but there is something inconstant in this partnership. It may be that the feelings run hot and cold, or that circumstances are such that their romantic feelings for one another are interrupted often. Difficult aspect: It's too easy for this relationship to end up becoming manipulative and frustrating. They may find that they have a hard time accomplishing much on a practical level when together because they tend to enjoy spending leisure time together. A difficult union that can succeed, but could involve some distancing and dishonesty.

George Clooney & Amal Alamuddin & Stacy Keibler & Elisabetta Canalis

George Clooney (born May 6, 1961; Lexington, KY; TAURUS, AQUARIUS moon) is married to Amal. (February 3, 1978; AQUARIUS, SAGITTARIUS moon), and these two are fairly compatible, however their stubborn TAURUS/AQUARIUS sun signs may be difficult at times. If at first the relationship is charming and agreeable, it will quickly end up disharmonious and life together will become unbearable. If one of the two does not make an effort, or does not find a compromise, it leads irrevocably to a breakup. It's not only about love, it's about "like". It would be a good idea to schedule plenty of leisure time together, especially when other problems arise in the relationship, if only to remind each other how much they truly enjoy each other's company, tastes, and interests. They go well together, they love each other, and feel good, happy and radiant in each other's company. There is much attraction. They are capable of charming each other. Sometimes, they gloss over problems and conflicts just in order to keep the peace, which is not a good idea in the long run. They can interrupt each other often. Problems can arise when one or the other finds their partner too blunt or too critical. When involved in a conversation, they can compete for the microphone. Conversations can be very lively, but may often escalate into arguments. George previously dated Stacy Keibler (born October 14, 1979; Baltimore, MD; LIBRA, LEO moon) and Elisabetta Canalis (born September 12, 1978; Sassari, Italy; VIRGO, CAPRICORN moon). I'd suspect that Stacy was too free-spirited for his EARTH side, while Elisabetta was too serious for his AIR moon – almost had all the right ingredients but not quite. Hopefully Amal's fun/unique AIR side will work with this AIR moon.

Olivia Munn & Aaron Rodgers

Olivia (June 3, 1980; Oklahoma City, OK; GEMINI, AQUARIUS moon) is dating NFL QB Aaron Rodgers (born December 2, 1983; Chico, CA; SAGITTARIUS, SCORPIO moon). Their personalities match up, but Aaron's passionate Scorpio moon may be too much for Olivia. Here is a couple that may have frequent disputes, as they may find it difficult to speak calmly. Conflict is caused if they both want to dominate the other, and if they do not consciously attempt to relate on the basis of mutual understanding. The sexual attraction is unique and powerful at first, seeming to arise suddenly and unexpectedly. However, it is a temperamental attraction and can leave just as suddenly.

Neil Patrick Harris & David Burtka

NPH (born June 15, 1973; Albuquerque, NM; GEMINI, SAGITTARIUS moon) is married to David (born May 29, 1975; Dearborn, MI; GEMINI, AQUARIUS moon) and make a darn superb match, no worries here. They are able to solve problems when they put their heads together. Respect for each other's intelligence. Good understanding between the two persons and intellectual interests in common. Similar or harmonious type of curiosity. A relationship which will be agreeable, they will like to speak to each other, have a good intellectual understanding, their tastes will be very similar, they will like to share their feelings with each other. They can interrupt each other often. Problems can arise when one or the other finds their partner too blunt or too critical. When involved in a conversation, they can compete for the microphone. Conversations can be very lively, but may often escalate into arguments.

Jennifer Lawrence & Nicholas Hoult

Jennifer (born August 15, 1990; Louisville, KY; LEO, GEMINI moon) is dating Nicholas (born December 7, 1989; Berkshire, England; SAGITTARIUS, ARIES moon), and these two make an awesome pair, based on their charts. A life together that can be very challenging at times on an intellectual level. Intellectual misunderstandings, diametrically opposed tastes, different ideas. Their styles in expressing love, and their preferred way to receive love, are at odds. This can be a real nuisance because there can be a lot of misunderstandings and wasted energy trying to explain oneself. They often feel let down with one another, usually because each wants very much to please the other, but it is hard to fulfill all the promises that are made to one another.

Jessica Simpson & Eric Johnson & Nick Lachey & Vanessa Minnillo

Jessica (born July 10, 1980; Abilene, TX; CANCER, GEMINI moon) is married to Eric (born September 15. 1979; Needham, MA; VIRGO, CANCER moon). This is a union that is particularly based on physical understanding, passionate love. There is a lot of affection between them, and they need to express it physically. Plenty of attraction here. They are able to solve problems when they put their heads together. Respect for each other's intelligence. Good understanding between the two persons and intellectual interests in common. Similar or harmonious type of curiosity. Great passionate affair, very intense and transforming. They feel that the relationship forces them to grow. Jessica was previously married to Nick Lachey (born November 9, 1973; Harlan, KY; SCORPIO, TAURUS moon), who is now married to Vanessa Minnillo (born November 9, 1980; Pampanga, Philippines; SCORPIO, SCORPIO moon). It makes sense why Nick and Jessica didn't work out – they may have WATER in them, but his EARTH probably was too much for her AIR moon, just not compatible in the relationship, whereas Eric's more sensitive CANCER moon probably gives into Jessica more so (than Nick's TAURUS!). And Vanessa and Nick are a great match with lots of WATER in their charts. It's an excellent aspect for a union because neither has to explain to the other about his or her life goals and overall personality. The two people complement each other in basic ways. Although every relationship has its struggles and conflicts, this aspect helps strengthen your relationship because there is an overall understanding and you support one another at the end of the day.

Goldie Hawn & Kurt Russell

Goldie Hawn (born November 21, 1945; Washington, D.C.; SCORPIO, GEMINI moon) has been with Kurt Russell (born March 17, 1951; Springfield, MA; PISCES, CANCER moon) for over 30 years, and you can see why, with all their WATER compatibility. Although every relationship has its struggles and conflicts, this aspect helps strengthen your relationship because there is an overall understanding and you support one another at the end of the day. They stimulate each other to be more creative and expressive. They learn a great deal from each other. They understand each other, like to discuss things with each other and undertake joint initiatives. Great intellectual understanding. Here is a couple you can call stable. They will lead their life together quietly, with friendship slowly replacing love. Enormous physical passion. The sexual attraction is intense and insistent. They want to be around each other as much as possible. Their sexual relationship evolves with time, instead of dissolves. Favorable union of the minds. They speak to each other about things they never talk about to others.

Adam Levine & Behati Prinsloo & Anne V

Adam (born March 18, 1979; Los Angeles, CA; PISCES, SCORPIO moon) is married to Behati (born May 16, 1989; Grootfontein, South-West Africa; TAURUS, LIBRA moon). He previously dated supermodel Anne V (born March 19, 1986; Gorky, Soviet Union; PISCES, CANCER moon). Anne V was probably more of a better fit on paper, but LIBRA moons are great companions for any partner because they prefer being in a relationship. His Scorpio moon requires nothing less than 100% loyalty and devotion. It's an excellent aspect for a union because neither has to explain to the other about his or her life goals and overall personality. The two people complement each other in basic ways. Although every relationship has its struggles and conflicts, this aspect helps strengthen your relationship because there is an overall understanding and you support one another at the end of the day. They have good intentions towards each other, but they often promise more than they can deliver. They make big plans that often fail to be realized. When one person wants to spend "together time," the other feels restless and dreams of being somewhere else. Freedom versus closeness is a conflict that arises often in this relationship. Favorable for all types of communication. It is so easy to get the ideas flowing. Great mental energy between the two. They respect each other's minds. Positive aspect: A life together in which each will desire the other and satisfy each other's sexual needs. Frustration levels tend to be minimal, and this helps the couple develop a pleasant atmosphere between them. They may do great things together or simply inspire one another.

Charlize Theron & Sean Penn

Charlize (born August 7, 1975; Benoni, South Africa; LEO, LEO moon) is dating Sean Penn (born August 17, 1960; Los Angeles, CA; LEO, CANCER moon). Hopefully their LEO sides don't compete too much with one another, but I could see Sean being much more sensitive in love, while Charlize may require more attention. Here is a couple that may have frequent disputes, as they may find it difficult to speak calmly. They might too frequently adopt an aggressive, defensive, or offensive stance with one another. Conflict is caused if they both want to dominate the other, and if they do not consciously attempt to relate on the basis of mutual understanding. One may lay down the law, give orders, and make decisions and the other may be an independent type, who cannot stand being limited or taking orders. A love that is particularly based on physical understanding, a passionate love with all its negative sides: possessiveness, jealousy, aggressiveness. Such a union is unlikely to last, but if it does, there are a lot of hurt feelings and stormy confrontations. The sexual attraction is especially strong at the beginning, but disagreements often have a major impact on the sex life. They end up on opposite ends of the couch frequently. The attraction is certainly there, but the relationship can lose its innocence quite easily. Positive aspect: This union can be favorable, if the two mutually respect each other. They both like their independence, their freedom of thought and action.

Justin Bieber & Selena Gomez

Justin (born March 1, 1994; Ontario, Canada; PISCES, SCORPIO moon) was dating Selena Gomez (born July 22, 1992; Grand Prairie, TX; LEO, ARIES moon) and were not at all compatible. Good thing they broke up. He was probably way too emotional for her rational side. Life together, if this happens, will be full of aggression and conflict. Not always the best of unions. They don't always share the same ideas, their tastes are different and this leads to a few tense moments due to lack of understanding. While they get on well when they first meet, sharing the same ideas and tastes, with the years, their ideas change and they do not develop in the same way. They will no longer understand each other and could split up because they no longer love each other, have nothing more in common. Sexual passion leading to destruction. It will be very difficult to pick oneself up after such a relationship. If it ends, there are likely to be hard feelings.

Blake Lively & Ryan Reynolds & Scarlett Johansson

Blake (born August 25, 1987; Tarzana, CA; VIRGO, VIRGO moon) is married to Ryan (born October 23, 1976; Vancouver, Canada; SCORPIO, SCORPIO moon). He was previously married to Scarlett Johansson (born November 22, 1984; New York, NY; SAGITTARIUS, SCORPIO moon). Interestingly they both have doubles of their signs, so it makes them more unique, or perhaps they just stand out more as their signs! Her EARTH is compatible with his WATER. It's an excellent aspect for a union because neither has to explain to the other about his or her life goals and overall personality. The two people complement each other in basic ways. Although every relationship has its struggles and conflicts, this aspect helps strengthen their relationship because there is an overall understanding and they support one another at the end of the day. Negative aspect: The two persons are drawn towards each other, but the union is unstable because there will inevitably be division, probably through misunderstanding on the sexual level, which may frustrate the partner. While they get on well when they first meet, sharing the same ideas and tastes, with the years, their ideas change and they do not develop in the same way. They will no longer understand each other and could split up because they no longer love each other, have nothing more in common. Positive aspect: Pure sexual attraction can unite the couple. They feel as if they have an ideal partner. They will be energetic, full of life and can undertake things together on a professional level or travel together on adventurous, unpredictable journeys. They respect each other's goals and drives, and don't stand in the way of their attempts to achieve their goals. Their body rhythms match well, and they share a basic physical bond that is hard to break. Energizing.

Oprah Winfrey & Stedman Graham & Gayle King

Oprah (born January 29, 1954; Kosciusko, MS; AQUARIUS, SAGITTARIUS moon) has been with her partner Stedman (born March 6, 1951; Whitesboro, NJ; PISCES, PISCES moon) for over 27 years. She definitely wears the pants in this relationship, as he is very passive (PISCES). A tendency to want to direct the partner's thoughts and ideas. Reading too much into what is said and what is not said. This union can be favorable, if the two mutually respect each other. They both like their independence, their freedom of thought and action. Favorable union, linking invention and originality with common sense and thoughtfulness. They will do great things together. Her best friend is Gayle King (born December 28, 1954; Chevy Chase, MD; CAPRICORN, AQUARIUS moon) and Gayle might be a little more serious/practical, but their AQUARIUS features probably keep them together – both being humanitarians and fighting for justice!

Pink & Carey Hart

Pink (born September 8, 1979; Abington Township, PA; VIRGO, ARIES moon) is married to Carey Hart (born March 13, 1975; Seal Beach, CA; PISCES, ARIES moon) and definitely seem like a good pair, especially with their similar moons. This relationship can only bring illusions, and therefore also disappointments will follow. These two people can never understand each other and if they insist on living together, it will be with lies and deception. Pure sexual attraction can unite the couple. They feel as if they have an ideal partner. They will be energetic, full of life and can undertake things together on a professional level or travel together on adventurous, unpredictable journeys. They respect each other's goals and drives, and don't stand in the way of their attempts to achieve their goals. Their body rhythms match well, and they share a basic physical bond that is hard to break. Energizing. The two persons are drawn towards each other, but the union is unstable because there will inevitably be division, probably through misunderstanding on the sexual level, which may frustrate the partner. Positive aspect: This union is likely to be completely successful. A couple that is happy to be alive, and to live together, with a pleasant family and home, total confidence in each other (and with reason), intellectual understanding and similar tastes. There is a strong desire to make each other happy. Forgiveness and graciousness characterizes their partnership.

Bill & Hillary Rodham Clinton & Monica Lewinsky

Bill (born August 19, 1946; Hope, AR; LEO, TAURUS moon) is married to Hillary (born October 26, 1947; Chicago, IL; SCORPIO, PISCES moon). They are certainly not made to live together. Favorable union, they have the same artistic tastes in common, their life will sometimes be full of fantasy. Favorable union, linking invention and originality with common sense and thoughtfulness. They will do great things together. This is not a defining element of compatibility, but it is supportive. They both like their independence, their freedom of thought and action. He had a famous affair with Monica Lewinsky (born July 23, 1973; San Francisco, CA; LEO, TAURUS moon). Did you notice the similar profiles between Bill and Monica? That could explain a lot. I think Hillary is a lot more focused and passionate about politics (SCORPIO) than Bill's LEO side, which makes him a great leader, but he may crave attention a little too much (hence the famous affair).

Rihanna & Drake

Rihanna (born February 20, 1988; Saint Michael, Barbados; PISCES, ARIES moon) has been linked to dating Drake (but are no longer) (born October 24, 1986; Ontario, Canada; SCORPIO, CANCER moon), and they both have a lot of WATER, however, he may be more attached emotionally than her FIRE moon will allow. Note: her former man Chris Brown is a double TAURUS, which explains a lot – much more stubborn, and a TAURUS and ARIES are not at all compatible (Ram vs. Bull). However, for Rihanna and Drake, it's an excellent aspect for a union because neither has to explain to the other about his or her life goals and overall personality. The two people complement each other in basic ways. Although every relationship has its struggles and conflicts, this aspect helps strengthen their relationship because there is an overall understanding and they support one another at the end of the day. They stimulate each other to be more creative and expressive. They learn a great deal from each other. They understand each other, like to discuss things with each other and undertake joint initiatives. Great intellectual understanding.

Kate Hudson & Matthew Bellamy & Chris Robinson

Kate Hudson (born April 19, 1979; Los Angeles, CA; ARIES, CAPRICORN moon) is engaged to Matthew Bellamy (born June 9, 1978; Cambridge, England; GEMINI, CANCER moon). She was previously married to Chris Robinson (born December 20, 1966; Marietta, GA; SAGITTARIUS, ARIES moon). Matthew may be more sensitive for her (WATER side), but lacks the EARTH element, as did Chris. So, hopefully he has other parts that might be more compatible for Kate's FIRE and EARTH sides. They have good intentions towards each other, but they often promise more than they can deliver. They make big plans that often fail to be realized. When one person wants to spend "together time," the other feels restless and dreams of being somewhere else. Freedom versus closeness is a conflict that arises often in this relationship. It's love-at-first-sight, the great passion: they will be drawn to each other like two magnets, they will always have to see and touch each other. They have a very good sexual understanding, typically very passionate. It must be said that this type of relationship may not last forever; it may not develop into a quiet and tender love. If they part, it is close to impossible to stay friends because of the constant reminder of the passion that once existed. It's all or nothing with them. If they part, one will suffer when the passion of the other dies, it will be a very difficult time to live through. However, if they stay together, there is strength to gain from each other. Union or love will be very strong, not at all intellectual, but sensual and full of romanticism and originality.

BIG BANG THEORY (SEASON 1, EP 16)

Leonard: How did you know my birthday's Saturday?

Penny: I did your horoscope, remember? I was going to do everybody's until Sheldon went on one of his typical psychotic rants.

Sheldon Cooper: For the record, that psychotic rant was a concise summation of the research of Bertram Forer, who, in 1948, proved conclusively through meticulously designed experiments that astrology is nothing but pseudoscientific hokum.

Penny: Blah, blah, blah, a typical Taurus.

Chapter 6
Political Recipes

"I do not believe in Astrology; but then, people of my sign never do."

Dr. Charles Tart, psychologist
(DOB: April 29, 1937; TAURUS)

I think with the past 2012 election, it's interesting to look at zodiac signs among our current and past President candidates. Some questions have come up in the past year when I was looking into Zodiacs. For me, I kept wondering if Republicans are more likely to be EARTH and WATER signs vs. Democrats who are more likely to be AIR and FIRE signs? What are most of our U.S. Presidents' signs? And then, what are the 2008 and 2012 election breakdowns of signs? However, I am still perplexed by the correlation among zodiacs and politics, something I will continue researching. Let's discuss these next. Read more on politics and astrology, especially in regards to predictions for the 2012 Presidential election: http://politicalastrology blog.com/2012/04/29/prediction-for-the-2012-us-presidential-election/

Birth times for all candidates: http://politicalastrologyblog.com/2011/05/22/status-of-the-2012-presidential-candidates-birth-times/

2012 ELECTION

President Barack Obama: Born August 4th 1961 (LEO; GEMINI moon; AQUARIUS ascendant) in Honolulu, Hawaii, 7:24 pm.

Here is his full birth chart --

Sun in Leo: Leos do feel important, but this generally takes the form of wanting to change the world in some way--to make the world a better place. They are generally motivated by affection for people, and often have big dreams and plans to make people happy. Generally, Leos are hard-working.

After all, they are attracted to the good things in life, and they know they have to work to get them. When they do get to work, they do it with intensity and determination. In this way, they are not unlike their symbol, the lion. The worst thing you can do to a Leo is accuse them of bad intentions. Displaying behavior that makes them think you don't appreciate them runs a close second. These happy, jovial people become mighty hurt when others don't see them for their noble intentions. Loyal, and sometimes rather traditional, Leos are, after all, a fixed sign. They'll hold onto situations and people for a very long time before they give up. There is an unmistakable idealism to Leo's view of the world and the people in it. Often, Leos have a very noble inner code that they answer to. Although on the surface, Leos appear rather confident, they can actually be some of the most humble souls around. They are the first to blame themselves when something goes wrong. Once again, it's the Leonine self-importance at work, and this characteristic works in unexpected ways. Instead of being the conceited, self-absorbed show-offs of reputation, they are usually very self-aware, self-conscious, and, yes, even humble.

Short description: He is masterful, likes authority, and aspires towards an ideal. He likes to give advice. He is honest, frank, loyal, open, and sincere.

Weaknesses: pride, vanity, arrogance, presumption, and disdain of others.

Leo ascendant Aquarius: The work that they do, and the services that they offer, are very important to their sense of identity. In order to feel good about themselves, they need to be busy with daily activities and to produce work they can be proud of. They need to focus on finding a suitable and rewarding avenue for expressing this part of themselves, being extra careful to choose an occupation in which they can express themselves. They are sensitive to criticism about the work they do, and they work best when they can create their own schedule. Positive feedback for the services they render is important to them, but they need to be careful not to over-identify with the appreciation they receive from others, as their work and health suffers when they feel under-appreciated. Motivation to do a good job should come from within.

They have a desire to be something special or to experience something more than the ordinary. They are day-dreamers and idealist. It is easy for them to trust others, even (and perhaps especially) people who might seem from the outside looking in as unsavory types. They are looking to identify with something beyond what is normally expected of people. They may have had a childhood that didn't help them direct or define their life. Perhaps the early family life was lacking in supervision or clearly defined rules. *A father figure may have been absent or distant and ineffective*. They may have a glorified image of their father. Whether the image is very positive or very negative (or if it swings between these extremes), the image is not very clear or rational. Whatever the case may be, *they struggle with defining who they are*. They might gravitate towards the "wrong people," or get in with the "wrong crowd" in an attempt to define who they are. They might be susceptible to being taken advantage of by others, especially by men or authority figures. They may be easily led astray by peculiar desires or self-destructive habits. In order to add a greater-than-ordinary dimension of experience to their life that helps them to feel special and important, they might be attracted to Neptune-ruled behaviors, such as secret affairs, drugs, or other escapist behaviors. In some way, they may feel a strong urge to glamorize their role in the world. There can be some confusion about the past (such as remembering childhood experiences in ways that are far removed from reality), and a tendency to daydream about being someone more "important" than they feel they are. They may struggle with early conditioning that made them feel tossed aside or neglected in some way, and certainly not directed or supported. They are very sensitive, especially with regards to any real or imagined blows to their ego. If the natal chart shows a strong sense of reality and a robust mind (Mercury and Saturn well-placed, for example), the negative interpretations of this aspect are less extreme. Still, they are likely to recognize at some point in their life that theu have a tendency to engage in escapist and self-destructive fantasies and/or habits. It is useful to be able to connect these behaviors with their probable source, which is likely to be a weakly-defined ego and identity in childhood.

He can face conflicts in life due to a projection of character that doesn't match what is on the inside. Misrepresentation of the self is frequent. He must strive to understand how others perceive him and work on presenting a more accurate persona to the world, or he will rub people the wrong way or feel unrecognized and misunderstood.

<u>Moon in Gemini</u>: Lunar Geminis are usually pleasant, witty, and charming people. At home and with family, however, they can be moody and irritable at times. People with Moon in Gemini are always interesting people--they have a finger in every pie, are curious to a fault, and are generally well-informed. Nervousness and worry are common traits with this lunar position. An underlying restlessness

is common, and many Lunar Geminis need more stimulation than others. They usually read a lot, talk a lot, and think a lot with this airy, mutable position of the Moon. Their homes are often a perpetual work-in-progress. They generally dislike housework, but are big on home improvement. Re-organizing their homes in little--and sometimes big--ways seems to keep them happy, as Lunar Geminis are easily bored by both routine and constancy. Often, this is a reflection of their inner world--"the grass is always greener..." applies here. Inwardly, Lunar Geminis are often unsettled. Moon in Gemini parents are generally more adept at handling the intellectual needs of their children than emotional ones. Others' complicated emotions, in general, can be difficult for Lunar Geminis to handle. In their families, Lunar Geminis often take on the role of organizing get-togethers. They are at their best when they have plenty of things to do beyond routine. Moon in Gemini people almost always have a way with words. They are clever and witty, and more often than not can be found chatting with others. They are sociable and friendly, and feel comfortable in crowds. Some pay too much attention to what everyone else is doing, and lose touch with what they really want to do. Generally, Lunar Geminis have a million and one projects going. They are impressionable folk, and their imagination is boundless. Their openness to new ideas is admirable, although decisiveness and persistence take a blow as a result. Still, versatility and adaptability are some of the stronger traits of this position of the Moon. When irritable, these people can easily become snappy. Their moodiness is complicated--this is not the same kind of moodiness you'll find with water sign moons, for example. Usually, difficult behavior stems from inner restlessness. Lunar Geminis want to do it all, and have trouble sticking to any one project. When problems arise, the first instinct of Moon in Gemini natives is to talk things out. Their tendency to analyze can give them the appearance of emotional detachment. In fact, Lunar Geminis may be especially comfortable talking about their feelings, but feeling their own feelings doesn't come as easily. Those that don't take time out to really emote and understand their own needs may end up baffling others. Feeling misunderstood is common for Moon in Gemini natives. The only real solution to the problem is learning to get in touch with their own feelings.

Short description: Sharp intellect. He likes literature, adapts to all situations and social groups. Work in contact with the public, literary occupations, travel.

Weaknesses: Lack of follow-up of ideas, indecision, goes back on decisions.

He likes family life, peace and quiet -- he likes to stay at home, surrounded by loved ones, in agreeable circumstances. **Strongly influenced by the mother.** You long for a sense of true belonging, but you may be quite restless in your search. You might change residence frequently, or simply feel the need to make many changes in your home. Moving frequently may be a healthy thing if it keeps you emotionally stimulated, but if you find that you do so on whims and later regret the changes, you might want to treat it as a symptom of emotional unrest--as a sign that you are in a constant search for the perfect mood and setting, when in fact a feeling of belonging should be worked on from the inside out, not the outside in! Some of you might remain rather immature on an emotional level, never wanting to truly grow up and take care of yourself. Attachments to your past, traditions, and family are strong.

He can be quite expressive and animated in his speech. He has an outstanding memory and tends to pick up a lot of information from his environment. He loves to chat and exchange ideas. Even if he is shy, once you're friends, he loves to talk about pretty much anything under the sun, and he enjoys sharing stories from his past! For the most part, he is focused on day-to-day activities in his communications rather than on grander philosophies. He is naturally curious and interested, and others find him very easy to talk to. He is accommodating and curious, but he is not as well equipped to handle heavy emotional demands. He thrives on change and variety. He might be a little addicted to gossip! More probable, however, he is simply very curious about others. There is a twinkle in his eyes, and he is never short on humor. He is playful and versatile--he makes a fun companion and an interesting friend. He listens! Yes, he does talk and occasionally interrupt in his excitement, but he is a curious person who does want to hear what others have to say, and that is a real pleasure. In fact, he is more able than most people to get others talking, simply because he is very receptive and sympathetic. He picks up others' feelings and body language readily.

He is generally pleasantly composed, due to an inner sense of harmony and emotional balance. He is optimistic--and realistically so, most of the time--which contributes to his overall "luck." He is able to get a real perspective on emotional matters that not only benefit his outlook, he is able to offer support to others when needed. Broad-mindedness is a wonderful characteristic. Quick to find humor in situations, he is generally warm and fun to be around. Deep down, he believes in the basic goodness of people and of life in general, and this basic and natural attitude helps him to attract positive circumstances and to make good connections. One of his best qualities is tolerance. Usually, he doesn't take life too seriously in the sense that he believes in having a bit of fun. His hunches are more often than not bang-on. He is frank, honest, optimistic, and generous. He likes good cooking, his comforts. His friendships are sincere. He is a worker and knows how to surround himself with the right people. He is appreciated at work.

He has intense emotions and passionate feelings. He fears the loss of control of emotional and domestic matters, and fears change. At the same time, he attracts change and disruptions. The love life or marital life may be riddled with emotional scenes, jealousy, and possessiveness because he attracts intense partners.

He has an irresolute nature, with sudden changes of humor. He is unstable and does not follow through on his own objectives. This instability shows itself not only in professional life, but also in love life and friendships.

Mercury in Leo: He wants to know the bottom line, and is good at scoping out a situation and finding answers to problems. In fact, he is a problem-solver, and will spend a lot of time helping others solve problems if need be. Very friendly and usually positive, he can be charming in a warm way. **Enthusiastic speaker, speaks with authority and sincerity.** Great sense of organization. Playful. Likes to take risks in jest and for amusement. Might sometimes come across too strongly or offend sensitive folk with a somewhat authoritative tone.

Medical profession. Serviceable and generous nature. Meets their soul sister at work, or (if not) through family contacts. He is a person who thinks of all the details that others forget. His mind is almost always turned "on" which can make him a little nervous. He is excellent at sorting things out, organizing, and making lists and associations. With his attention to the details and the mechanics, however, he might miss the bigger point! He is exceptionally helpful and others can count on him for making arrangements, researching, and offering advice. He truly loves to feel useful. He might have some traits of a hypochondriac, as he notices all of the little aches and pains that others might overlook. Nervous tension could be at the root of many of his health complaints. Many of them are good at crafts, mechanics, or anything that requires good manual dexterity.

He is frivolous and imprudent. He lacks judgment, and is full of self-importance. He has difficulty in realizing his plans because he lacks clarity and rates his qualities higher than they are. He is reserved, conservative, ambitious and stubborn. He might have problems expressing himself, particularly verbally, due to shyness or fear of criticism. Social success may be slow and laborious, but he does not give up easily and is patient. Whatever you say and write is self-censored to some degree. It's hard for you to pour out your emotions, no matter how emotional or needy you feel on the inside. This is because you are always aware of what others might think of you with what you say. You are careful with what you reveal to others. You make plenty of disclaimers, and often come across as negative or sarcastic without intending to. You often review conversations you have had with others, and you often kick yourself for saying something you didn't intend to, or for not saying something witty. There can be some feelings of insecurity about how you speak and communicate in general. Self-consciousness and hypersensitivity is experienced with regards to your intelligence and/or ability to get ideas across to others, especially in youth. You need plenty of positive feedback from others in order to feel more confident and less "blocked." Recognize that you are most likely harder on yourself about how you communicate than others are. Ask people close to you for an objective point of view. Chances are, they find you to be astute, intelligent, and an effective speaker or writer. We often tell our kids, "Don't worry about what others think," but telling this to a person with a hard Saturn aspect is not enough, nor is it realistic. They will worry. You rarely accept compliments whole-heartedly, yet you crave them and need them. Others around you tend to stop complimenting you, feeling that you either don't need compliments or don't want to hear them. Nothing can be further from the truth!

He likes to have his own ideas about things, to form an opinion and think over the problems it poses. He is an intellectual.

Venus in Cancer: Love for Venus in Cancer is best when it is committed and rather predictable. These people are sensitive in love, even if their Sun sign is the more playful and outgoing signs of Gemini or Leo. You may even say their egos are a little underdeveloped when it comes to love, but they have a lot to give in return: namely, security, comfort, and care. Venus in Cancer men and women show their love by caring for you. They pay more attention to your feelings than your words, and observe you rather carefully. They want a safe, solid relationship. They can be a little moody in love, and some go so far as giving silent treatments and engaging in pouting routines to get attention from their mate. They are turned off by anything impersonal, and too much rationalizing leaves them cold. They are not afraid of emotional confrontations (even if they have a Gemini Sun and appear flighty in other areas of life). Still, these lovers are always worried they'll be left high and dry. If you've hurt them, they'll have a hard time forgetting. Every so often, they'll retreat into themselves (not unlike a Crab), and it can be difficult to pull them out. This is when they use their extraordinary "nursing" abilities on themselves, instead of you...and you simply don't want that! Pleasing Venus in Cancer involves lots of snuggling and sentimentality. Recognize their attachments to their family and home. Help them to feel confident with you -- when they are fearful of being rejected, they can resort to some frustrating tactics to find out just how loved they are. Think about how a crab (the symbol of Cancer) moves towards its goal, and you will get a fair idea of Venus in Cancer's approach. Do your best to make them feel secure and cared for, and you will be rewarded with a patient, dependable, and loving mate.

He wants to succeed in his love-life. He meets pleasant people and has very good friends, usually without too much conflict. He likes amusements, parties. He may have many children. Interest in the opposite sex for he started young. Playful, sensual, and amorous, he is in love with love! He thrives on romantic attention, and it is easy and natural for him to always have a crush or romantic interest. There is a romantic, playful side to him that is unmistakable. It keeps him young at heart! He is sensuous and enjoys indulging in the pleasurable senses to the fullest possible extent. He enjoys surrounding himself with beautiful art and music, and these may play a role in his ideal date scenario. There is a touch of the dramatic in him when it comes to love and sex. He is generally quite loyal to his partner, and he is both charming and easily charmed. It's also easy to turn his head. He is a warm, fun and playful date.

His professional life is unstable. He has a taste for the Arts, is a dreamer, is easily influenced and romantic. He is emotional and very sensitive. Romantic, creative, gentle, and adaptable, he naturally expresses the finer qualities of mysterious and dreamy Neptune in his love relationships. His imagination is rich and his fantasy world well-developed. He is turned off by rudeness and crudeness, and are drawn to beauty in its many forms. He is very giving and generous, but may be a little on the submissive side, or sometimes downright lazy, failing to take the initiative when situations call for it.

<u>Mars in Virgo</u>: These productive and busy people are goal-oriented and practical. Although they can be a little scattered at times, simply because they are doing so many things at any given time, Mars in Virgo natives get things done--quite well! *They have a knack for handling a wide variety of tasks at once, and a tendency to take on perhaps too much at the same time.* Most Mars in Virgo natives are not particularly aggressive by nature. Although they can be a little hard-nosed and critical at times, they rarely resort to pushing others around. Still, an annoyed Mars in Virgo native can be difficult to be around! Arouse their anger and they turn into complaining, over-critical nags. Generally, these natives don't make themselves nuisances, so this stage is unlikely to last for very long. It is a sensitive position, however. It doesn't take much to make these people nervous. Mars in Virgo people are quite protective about their "system" for getting things done. Although rather humble in a general life sense, they can be quite particular about their methods-- how they organize and accomplish their goals, mostly with work. Theirs is a nervous energy. Although they have some staying power, they can be restless and are not given to sticking with the same projects for too long. These natives derive plenty of energy and life force from the things they do--their work, hobbies, and any kind of projects they take on. An idle Mars in Virgo native is a sorry sight, indeed. Fidgety, nervous, worried...all of these things are a sure sign that Mars in Virgo people have either too little to do, or far too much on their plates. There is a perfectionist at the heart of all people with this position. They'll be the first to deny this, but it's there! They worry when they are not producing anything, and they worry about whether what they've produced will measure up. An earthy and sometimes nervous sexuality generally characterizes people with this position of Mars. In a sense, their performance in bed is similar to their work. These people want to be good at what they do. They will generally be open to experimentation, if only to feed their curiosity and to feel savvy. There's often a shy and humble side to Mars in Virgo in any area that involves putting themselves out there and letting go (areas ruled by Mars). But experience and knowledge are important to these natives, and this drive generally wins over their natural reticence.

He dominates his associates, colleagues. He is the same in love life, dominating the spouse and this makes for a stormy relationship in prospect. He is energetic and determined. He has strength and resistance, ability and patience; he is tough, and sometimes insensitive, and puts all his energy and talents into overcoming all the obstacles to his success. He is obstinate, calculating, does not take on anything without having thought of all the possible consequences. He can take all the time in the world and never loses patience to achieve his objectives. He is not particularly popular in his circle, but is feared and respected.

<u>Jupiter in Aquarius</u>: *He attracts the most good fortune when he is tolerant and fair, inventive, impartial, and cooperative. He values people and personal freedom most. Wants to show unique perspective or skills. Open to new methods and progress. Great tolerance and humanitarianism.*

He is kind, and does charity work. He is protected from life's rigors to which he is not immune, but he knows how to cope. He likes working in peace and alone. He is serious, patient, honest, hard working, and orderly. His judgment is good and he thinks things over. He pursues his objectives to the bitter end, usually knowing when to choose the right moment. *He is upright and respects the law.*

He is a high liver, likes to have fun but knows what he wants and does whatever is necessary to get it. *He wants to - and does - succeed socially.* After a hard day's work, a good well-lubricated meal in the company of friends is just the ticket.

<u>Saturn in Capricorn</u>: He is scrupulous, honest, correct, worthy, and respectable.

Weaknesses: melancholy, sullenness, disappointment, and bitterness.

He likes quiet and solitude above everything. He looks for work (or can work) alone, without being bothered. He hates chatting and outside noises. He is ambitious, but in a calculated, well-balanced way. He perseveres, is serious and orderly. He climbs the ladder slowly but surely; if need be, he is willing to change his ideas. He is wise and experienced.

<u>Uranus in Leo</u>: He is self-contained, resolute, tenacious. Likes freedom of action and independence.

His independence does not tolerate traditional marriage very well. If he does marry, he has little chance of finishing his days with the spouse, unless the partner gives him complete freedom. He needs a lot of freedom in his partnerships and do best in unconventional or nontraditional set-ups. He is likely to attract unusual, erratic people into his life, particularly in close relationships. He is inconstant, lacks control, and is nervous.

He cannot carry through his plans, schemes to the end. These are changeable. He lacks forethought, attention. He throws himself into things, more than reacts to them.

<u>Leo ascendant Aquarius</u>: How unique and original Aquarius rising natives come across! These individuals are just that -- individuals, and they won't let you forget that fact. Often turned to for advice, these natives *possess intellectual poise and savvy.* They often are curious, and quite learned, in both science and metaphysics-- *anything that involves advancement of the human race holds much appeal.* It's hard to shock an Aquarius rising. They've seen it all, or at least want you to think they have. In fact, they often enjoy shocking others. Not that they are flamboyant by nature, but they do like to, albeit quietly, get a rise out of others. Some natives born with Aquarius on their Ascendant can be quietly provocative and irreverent. Most people with this Ascendant are quite friendly and likable. Their personality quirks generally go over quite well with others. They generally give others quite a bit of freedom--accepting, as a rule, people from all walks of life as equals. And their somewhat cool and detached curiosity about all that goes on around them appeals to most. Curiously, Aquarius rising people can be a little standoffish while also coming across as humanitarian and kind. Often labeled as independent and original children, Aquarius rising natives often feel a little "different" or "special" throughout life. They often feel like they are on the outside looking in, and their ability to observe and deduce is often uncanny. *They're also adept at getting things to work, even when the parts that make up the whole seem like a puzzle with unusual pieces--especially when it comes to groups of people. This sets them apart as managers and team leaders.* The Ascendant often reveals physical mannerisms and even choice of dress, as it shows how people present themselves to the world. With Aquarius here, natives sometimes have a quirkiness to their manner, and some dress in a slightly offbeat manner--not enough to make them stand out like a sore thumb, but just enough to express their original temperament. Because these people seem so open to new ideas, it may be surprising when you encounter their decidedly stubborn streak. Aquarius is a fixed sign, after all. The ascendant sign shows how individuals react to new situations, and with Aquarius rising, there can be a resistance to change that seems to belie the native's generally progressive nature. There's a distinct inflexibility with Aquarian rising people, and sometimes, a tendency to want to force their opinions on others. With their eye to the future of mankind as a whole, some people born with an Aquarius Ascendant

overlook the more personal needs of the people closest to them. They are often attracted to partners who possess self-confidence.

Since this is a book regarding compatibility, let's take a moment to look at **Michelle Obama**'s zodiac: Born January 17, 1964 in Chicago, IL (CAPRICORN; PISCES moon). Michelle's earthy and practical sun sign most likely keeps Barack grounded with his expansive ideas. But they are not very compatible, as she is more sensitive emotionally than him, perhaps insensitive GEMINI moon. Thus he's ruled by FIRE and AIR, and she is ruled by EARTH and WATER, but perhaps there are other elements that are compatible.

Vice President Joe Biden:

Born November 20, 1942 (SCORPIO; TAURUS Moon); Scranton, PA, unknown time.

Joe Biden is married to **Jill Biden** (born June 5, 1951; GEMINI; GEMINI moon), and these two are not very compatible, but I would suspect that Joe has a GEMINI ascendant sign (since he likes to talk a lot!!) and that she probably has WATER or EARTH elements in her birth chart.

2012 President Elect Mitt Romney: Born March 12th, 1947 (PISCES; SCORPIO moon), Detroit, Michigan, 9:51 am

Short description: He is compassionate and sentimental. Spirit of self-sacrifice. Pisces can be extraordinarily successful when given the chance to express themselves.

Weaknesses: tendency to be led astray, lack of experience or inability to apply experience practically. Lethargy, over-sensitivity and emotionalism.

Mitt is married to **Ann Romney**, born April 16, 1949 (ARIES;

SAGITTARIUS moon). I would say that these two are not very compatible, perhaps depends on Ann's ascendant sign. She's more aggressive and probably wears the pants in this relationship with her FIRE signs, whereas Mitt is ruled by his WATER emotional signs.

2008 ELECTION Candidates

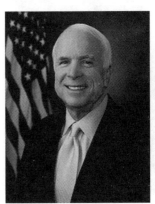

John McCain: Born August 29, 1936 (VIRGO; CAPRICORN moon); no time of birth; Panama Canal. John McCain is married to **Cindy McCain** (born May 20, 1954; TAURUS; CAPRICORN moon), both are extremely compatible and very EARTH driven and practical.

Sarah Palin: Born February 11th, 1964 (AQUARIUS; AQUARIUS moon), Sandpoint, Idaho, approximately 6 pm. Sarah is married to **Todd Palin** (born

September 6, 1964; VIRGO; VIRGO moon), and the only thing keeping these two together is her Ascendant sign of VIRGO (hopefully!), otherwise they are very incompatible.

2012 Republican Candidates

Michele Bachmann: Born April 6th, 1956, Waterloo, Iowa, 12:08 pm. (ARIES with an AQUARIUS moon sign). Married to Marcus Bachmann (DOB: unknown)

Herman Cain: Born December 13th, 1945, Memphis, Tennessee, unknown time. SAGITTARIUS with an ARIES moon.

Newt Gingrich: Born June 17th, 1943, Harrisburg, Pennsylvania, tentatively 11:45 pm; GEMINI with a SAGITTARIUS moon.

Jon Huntsman: Born March 26th 1960, Redwood City, California, 11:58 am; ARIES with an ARIES moon.

Ron Paul: Born August 20th, 1935, Pittsburgh, Pennsylvania, unknown time; LEO/VIRGO cusp with a TAURUS moon.

Tim Pawlenty: Born November 27th, 1960, Saint Paul, Minnesota, unknown time; SAGITTARIUS with an ARIES moon.

Rick Perry: Born March 4th 1950, Paint Creek, Texas, 10:40 am; PISCES with VIRGO moon.

Rick Santorum: Born May 10th, 1958, Winchester, Virginia, unknown time; TAURUS with an AQUARIUS moon.

Chapter 7
Pet Recipes

Ever wondered about your furry little creature? Perhaps why you really loved and connected with one pet more than another, or why some pets and owners clashed? Perhaps there's more to your pet than meets the eye. They have their own personalities, too. However, most pet owners do not know their pet's birthdays, which can be a real bummer. But, I challenge you to read below and decide what describes your pet best! And it may help in understanding, loving, and giving them the best life available.

ARIES pets need to be first! If you are looking for a pet that will become a champion, choose an Aries. They want to win at all costs and are the most competitive of all the signs. To win with these pets, let them think they are winning. Never fearful, these warriors will fight to the finish. Never one to hold a grudge, any display of anger will soon be forgotten. What you see is what you get in these guys. If you are liked they will protect you from harm, unless of course they feel they want to compete with you, then you are in trouble. They love a good fight and it might as well be with someone they like. Don't take offense, they are just being their true selves. Expect an exciting life with these little balls of fire. They are forever on the move and always looking for that next adventure. If you have more than one pet, your Arian will be the leader. Be careful, for they may be the leaders of your house, too! If they become bored, watch out. They will hunt up an adventure, so keep them busy, and give them lots of toys and creative competitive games to play. These guys love to play tug-of-war. Teach them early in life who is boss, otherwise you will be hiding from them. They cannot be easily put under leash. They call for attention. If not given adequate attention, they are likely to become rebellious, stubborn and disobedient. When pampered they do not hesitate to show back their gratitude. It is a little difficult to get them under your words. They are known to be territorial and defend the same with all their might. *Most desirable qualities*: Loyalty, trust, spontaneous, fearless; *Negative*: Impassive, risk taking, impatience; *Physical characteristics*: Active, energetic, prone to headaches and sun strokes.

TAURUS pets love the finer things in life. Give them the best seat in the house in front of the television. They will sit for hours just watching the TV with you. Hide that remote, for they want to be in control of that, too. In fact, they want to be in control of everything. Don't take their stuff, they will get crazy. Possessive little monsters, they may not want to eat any more in their bowl, but don't take it away until they deem it no longer theirs. Great little obedient pals, they will protect you as one of their own possessions. The original bull, which stands its ground when feeling threatened. If you are willing to allow them to move at a slow pace, they will do what is asked of them. Happiest when eating the finest foods. Watch their weight, as they do not know when to stop eating. They will eat everything they can get their little paws on. Once they park their little rears, they can't be moved until they are good and ready to move. If they find that most comfortable place on the couch, then they will possess that very spot for the rest of their days. You can be assured they will be just where you left them, if they feel comfortable. Sometimes mistaken for a piece of furniture, Taurus pets are known to be lazy ones! They tend to put on some weight with age. They are fond of gentle and warm surroundings. ***Most desirable qualities***: Steadfast, kind-hearted, stubborn, patient, affectionate, persistent; ***Negative***: Jealous, greedy, possessive, resentful; ***Physical characteristics***: Strong, powerful.

GEMINI pets are little talkers. If you like a nice peaceful environment, don't think you can have one with these little mouthpieces. These pets will report on the happenings of the neighborhood. Every person that walks by will be announced with a loud barking ruckus. Don't feel you are out of the woods if you own a cat. Cats can be just as verbal as dogs when it comes to expressing themselves. Sometimes these guys can be troublemakers. Your cat may not be the one causing the commotion, they may be sitting in the driveway looking innocent as the dogs across the street go crazy barking. A natural born instigator. When you have finally quieted them down, don't expect a quiet home. Now they will be running around the house for the sheer thrill of running. Don't worry that they will run far, these guys are sprinters and will only sprint in short bursts from room to room. They are very independent and want nothing to do with cuddling. They will come to you when it is in their mind to be petted and only the prescribed time. They like to entertain their masters and get the attention of outsiders easily. Gemini pets are charming, very domestic but sensitive, too. Usually curiosity gets them into unwanted troubles. They get along with any other pet and can also be trained easily as they are fast learners. ***Most desirable qualities***: Imaginative, expressive, restless, versatile, independent, curious; ***Negative***: Extrovert, inquisitive, loud, sometimes unaffectionate; *Physical characteristics*: Alert, graceful, energetic.

CANCER pets love their homes and family more than anything. They are the best watch protectors. They will protect their home from invaders. Try to get them out of the house for a walk. They would just love to sit in their homes and never leave. If you are looking for a pet for children, you have come across the right sign, they love children and babies. In fact, they will mother anything or anyone they can. Get them lots of toys that are soft and cuddly. If you don't have children they will cuddle pillows or your leg for that matter. If you like an independent animal you better get an Aquarius or Gemini. These guys won't let you go into another room without following you. "Velcro Pet" comes to mind when I think of Cancers. Depending on how big they are, you will have an animal always glued to your foot or ankle. Another eater. They love the sweets. If given too much, they will become little round balls of fat. Give them a cave to hide their toys in since they are collectors. If you must throw out one of their toys, don't let them see you. They could cry if they think you are giving away something they feel they own. Cancer pets are overly sensitive. They compel to be taken as one among your family members. If scolded they lose their mood and retreat to a corner. They crave for attention and if left unnoticed shall sulk and whine. Cancer cats are nocturnal ones and their mood changes with the phases of the moon. They never get into fights and are very timid. They run away from trouble and like to be pampered and cuddled by their owners. Cancer pets become friends for life. *Most desirable qualities*: Tenacious, sensitive, patient; *Negative*: Moody, needy; *Physical characteristics*: Long-legged.

LEO pets are the king of the jungle and your house. Better get some big mirrors so this King or Queen of the animals can bask in their own reflection. They love to be petted, admired, and generally treated like royalty. If you cannot give them your full attention they will need their favorite royal placement in the house. They prefer to be at the top, such as the couch, desk or chair. Make sure they are surrounded by lots of pillows because only kings deserve the best. This spot should be in the sun. Ruled by the sun, these guys do best on bright sunny days. Want to see what depression looks like? Don't turn on any lights, especially on a cold, rainy, winter day. They invented the word mopey for these types. Turn on the lights and warm up the room and what a transformation you will see. These pets are wonderful with other pets and people as long as they are the leader of the group. They will then make sure everyone is taken care of and part of the group. They cannot tolerate anyone being left out. They want and demand only the best. So if a guest has the warmest lap in town, they will end up there and no amount of persuading will change their minds for they are a stubborn lot as well. Leo pets are loving and faithful and demand their owner's attention 24 hours a day if there are other pets in the household. They have a good memory and make good pets particularly if there are small kids at home because they take good care of them. ***Most desirable qualities***: Faithful, loving, protective, playful; ***Negative***: Dominating, dramatic; ***Physical characteristics***: Well-proportioned body, graceful.

VIRGO pets are not fussy and are very clean. Anal Retentive fits them to a "T." Not very brave either, you could call these pets a wimp. On the other hand wimps can be a great pet to have around other pets. They won't fight for position. They will give into anyone who wants to be the top dog. They take very well to training. Routines give them lots of comfort. They like to do the same thing over and over again. Heaven forbid if you don't feed them exactly on time. You won't hear the end of it. Crying and howling come to mind if you decide to wait a half hour or so to feed them. Then is when your dear cat pushes your papers off your desk or sits down right in front of your computer screen until you perform your scheduled work duty. You have to watch their health, since they are very quick to get ill. Many times they won't even let you know until they are very sick. They hate to impose on others. But taking their vitamins and eating good food will help with their health. Their weakest area is their intestines so watch that they don't eat too many treats to clog up their very delicate body systems. Be careful of changing their diets, too, for once they are given a routine, they love the same food all the time. Virgo pets are very hygienic and demand a spick environment around them. They like to be clean always and are ready to take a bath any time of the day which most of the pets hate. Virgo pets are particularly demanding. They avoid working and prefer to play around most of the day. They make a big fuss around dinner time. They are not much fond of seeking attention. They are prone to allergies and hence maintain caution. A strict diet is to be followed for them or else they get an upset tummy. ***Most desirable qualities***: Affectionate, smart, outgoing, happy; ***Negative***: Cowardly, demanding ***Physical characteristics***: Strong, muscular.

LIBRA pets are the beauties of the zodiac, by far the prettiest pet. Not only in looks but very charming as well. They get what they want by persuading you to do something for them. They can be very lazy. Being lazy comes from the inability to make up their minds. They spend so much time on deciding, they get tired and want you then to do it for them. They really can see both sides of an issue, so to them anything is okay. You can then do it for them. If you chose correctly they will reward you with charm, if you did it incorrectly they will fight you. Just when you think you have these guys figured out, they change their minds. Like the Gemini and Aquarius, all three air signs, they do not like to be smothered. That is of course unless they have decided that is what they want. So be very patient and flexible with these pretty charmers for they will demand it of you. Libra pets communicate their feelings to the owner through their eyes. They are restless and indecisive creatures. They have finicky manners and test the patience of the owner. They shall do anything if they want to get attention. They are very affectionate and like the company of other pets as well in the house. They are known to be flirts and cannot be accommodated into a particular routine. Their nervous nature usually lands them in troubled waters. *Most desirable qualities*: Well-balanced, affectionate; *Negative*: Manipulative, indecisive, lazy; *Physical characteristics*: Well-nourished.

SCORPIO pets are the secret agents of the zodiac. You never know where your things are with this sign. They have so many hiding places you would be amazed. Whenever they are mad at you, you can expect your things to be taken and hidden. These are the cats that seem so innocent and yet your hair brush is gone for days and one day shows up in the toilet. Intensity is the name of this sign's game. Everything is a matter of grave importance or they won't do it. They love to play cat and mouse games. Anything where they can go for the kill is fun for them. This is the cat that brings home the dead creatures. If you try to make them do something they would prefer not to, then LOOK OUT! They won't go for that. One of the most stubborn signs of the zodiac, they will not be pushed into something they do not want. If you insist they do a dog obedience school, then watch out because these are the sneaky ones. You never really know with them. You can't tell what will anger them. Since they are a water sign, keeping a calm house would help lessen their intensity and prevent some of the drama these little Tasmanian devils are always into. But Scorpio pets are loyal and very entertaining. They keep their owners in a good mood. They are very much attached to home. They have the ability to read people's mind. They easily sense danger. They are loners and are rarely found inside the house. They live in a world of their own. *Most desirable qualities*: Independent, determined, playful, loyal; *Negative*: Jealous, resentful, obstinate, sneaky; *Physical characteristics*: Handsome features.

SAGITTARIUS pets are the travelers and teachers of the zodiac. They love to go out into the neighborhood and meet new people and animals. Watch to see they don't escape and run wild. They do love to be ahead of the others and demand attention. They only want attention when they want it. Sags are very independent and love to spend time alone being free. They hate to be tied down to family, house or yard. Give them lots and lots of freedom. If you have an active family with lots of boys who love to exercise, pick a Sag for your son. These guys love to catch balls, play tug-a-war, chase squirrels and generally love anything to do with activity. The perfect dog for learning tricks in a competition style atmosphere. On other days, these most active animals can be the laziest of the zodiac. They want to do only fun things. If you are wanting them to do something that they perceive as not, they will just lay down and not do it. If you have ever tried to give a cat a bath, this is the image you will get when you try to make a Sag pet do something they do not want to do. The fighter in them will become very apparent in a very short time. When they are in the mood, they find great pleasure in making others laugh. They can be very entertaining creatures. The jokester and court jester of the zodiac. They have long legs and love to run. Take them out for an hour run each day and they will love you for it. Sagittarius pets are full of boundless energy and with strong nerves. They are fun-loving creatures. Sagittarius pets are very good to keep at a young age. As they grow up they become temperate. They are also the most accident-prone members of the zodiac. They easily get into troubles because of their clumsy nature. They love to be loved and give back the same to their owner. Sagittarius pets are cowards and mostly run out of any serious fight. They like adventure. *Most desirable qualities*: Nature loving, active, jovial, companionship; *Negative*: Restless, quick-tempered, stubborn; *Physical characteristics*: Well-balanced body.

CAPRICORN pets are the workers of the zodiac who never give up. These hard working little guys are very stubborn and if they want something, they don't give up. Tenacious comes to mind when one thinks of Capricorn pets. If you have a dog, you will most likely have a digger. They love to dig holes. Being an earth sign they feel they must connect with the earth. What better way then to dig a hole. Here is another pet that loves routines. These pets will let you know when something is not as it should be. That could be a stranger at the door or his bed not set up properly. They will cry, whine or just keep at you until you change things the way he/she thinks they should be. Capricorn pets are found to be wiser when compared to the other pets of their age. They are also known for their proper behavior and keeping the house in order. Capricorn cats love to sleep endlessly. They put on weight as they have a bent on food. Capricorns are stubborn and hate to be disturbed from their place. They are said to be self-centered but hate to be alone. ***Most desirable qualities***: Reserved, ambitious, careful; ***Negative***: Stubborn, persistent; ***Physical characteristics***: Perfection in form and build.

AQUARIUS pets are the friendliest, and will bring home every other pet in the neighborhood. They love everyone and everything. Once they get the new friends home, it is up to you to entertain them and keep them. They have done their job when they bring in strays. Now you fix them up. When they are not busy with other pets, they can do very, very strange things. These are the pets of the weird and unusual. Just when you think they are going to do one thing, they change their mind and behave totally different. Never one for routine, these little guys change their behavior for the fun of it. Where Capricorns were great in school, these guys will defy anything that looks like restrictions; school or anything that might impede their freedom. Don't keep them restricted too long or they might find the need to leave you and find freedom in the world. Don't cuddle and pet them too much for they really don't like too much closeness. They need their freedom to be the unusual pet they are. Not one for being bored, they will stir up trouble just to see what will happen. Don't ever feed them the same thing twice. They will let you know when you have crossed that line and will become very disapproving when you do something that you have done before. Unusual and different are their key words. Being another Air sign they are talkers and very verbal. Look for them to be barkers and pets that express their needs all the time. Aquarius pets are gentle creatures. They sense the moods of their owners and act accordingly. They have a liking for water and taking them to a bath is very easy. They are very friendly and intelligent. Aquarius cats are very temperamental. Training them is not an easy affair. ***Most desirable qualities***: Determination, curiosity, devotion, independent; ***Negative***: Unpredictable, detached; ***Physical characteristics***: Slow, well-built, tall.

PISCES pets are the kindest and most caring of all the pets. They can feel your feelings almost better than you can. They seem to know your moods and react to them. These kind souls are often spacey beyond anything you have ever seen. They never seem to know where they are going or where they have been. Some of these pets can be so spacey they miss what is going on in the world. They are often the cats that spend hours staring at the wall. To soothe a Pisces, make sure they do not have too much stress or input from the outside world. They are easily excited and often take on the feelings of others and do not even know it has become part of their feelings. To really help these sensitive creatures, play music for them, but not too loud for they have sensitive ears, too. Speaking of ears, don't forget to check to see if they have ear mites or infections in those ears. They are prone to both. Piscean pets love water and related sports. They are very sensitive and emphatic and easily sense their owners' moods. Once they develop a liking for a particular person, they shall stick on for life. They are accident prone. Piscean cats are hyperactive and impulsive in nature. Piscean pets change their moods so often that it is difficult to understand them. They love luxury and do not need much space. A change of environment shall make them sulk to a corner. But for that they are gentle and loving pets. ***Most desirable qualities***: Mystical, kind, gentle; ***Negative***: Weak-willed, excitable, air-headed; ***Physical characteristics***: Athletic, lean.

Great Pet Zodiac websites:

http://www.findyourfate.com/astrology/pet-astrology.htm

http://www.psychicreadingswithmarie.com/pet-zodiac.php

The puzzling thing is that there is really a curious coincidence between astrological and psychological facts, so that one can isolate time from the characteristics of an individual, and also, one can deduce characteristics from a certain time....

~Carl Jung

EPILOGUE

Final Advice for you & your Relationship(s)

So what if you're in a current relationship that you very much enjoy (or hate?), and this book has told you that you are incompatible with your mate? Now what? Well, first of all, don't freak out, this isn't the entire recipe! There's so much more. Yes, you may not be compatible zodiac-wise, but it doesn't mean you can't work on the relationship. Don't make this a self-fulfilling prophecy, whereby you hear something bad about your relationship and you now think it's doomed. Not the case. It's more of a "now you know the weaknesses in your relationship that you can work on if you really want it to work out."

However, for those who are single, well then pay attention! When I first began researching this area, the joke with my friends was that I would always ask a potential mate or one of their potential mates "What's their birthday?" It was a running joke, but now I actually think it holds more water. That is honestly the first question I think of when meeting someone, and I hope you will, too! This, however, could be a potential bad thing, a bias if you will, but I also think it can give you an idea of who they might be before getting to know them further. In addition, it might save a lot of time "kissing a lot of frogs, before you meet the Prince." Now again, I repeat myself: Don't judge someone just by their birthday, there's a lot more to it (Moon, Planets, personality, love language, etc). And there are smart phones now that are useful – there are apps for checking a person's MOON SIGN for example (called "Moon Sign") and having internet on your phone makes it accessible to check a person's birth chart. However, it may not guarantee you another date if you ask someone on the first date "Hey, what's your birthday? Oh, and I need your time of birth and the location." Yes, you might want to wait to ask that very odd question for a little while.

In conclusion, this book is ultimately about helping you understand yourself a little better. A lot of you may be critics, which is completely understandable, and wondering "seriously, your birth time/date tells you everything you need to know about a person? Yeah right! The stars and moon are that important?" Well, I would argue, yes, they are important, but are just another element or factor to consider. I study human development, so I'll be the first to tell you that there are a number of factors that are important – where you're born (region/culture/community), your parents' environment and genetics, and even the generation you're born into and time in history. All these factors, along with zodiacs, make up the context that make you – well YOU! It makes you unique and may help explain a few additional things that you never knew. Just try reading your birth chart, even if you don't believe in it, you may learn a thing or two about yourself. And if you're still not convinced, well then you might just be a stubborn Taurus!

Astrology is a science in itself, and contains an illuminating body of knowledge. It has taught me many things, and I am greatly in debt to it."

Albert Einstein

About the Author

Dr. Jackie Wiersma currently resides in Fayetteville, AR where she teaches at the University of Arkansas. She is originally from Le Mars, IA where she did her Bachelor's in Psychology at the University of Northern Iowa. She then pursued graduate degrees with a Master's in Human Development & Family Sciences (HDFS) at Arizona State University, a Ph.D. in HDFS at Texas Tech University, and a post-doc at Penn State University. Jackie currently teaches a large Family Relations course at the U of A and has been studying young adult relationships for the past 10 years, with a curiosity in mate selection.

After moving to Arkansas four years ago, she became interested in the subject of astrology and zodiacs, based on her friends' birthdays and their own compatibilities. She soon became an expert on zodiacs and has written the book *"The Zodiac Recipe: A Ph.D.'s Guide to Understanding You and Your Relationships."*

Other Books By Ozark Mountain Publishing, Inc.

Dolores Cannon
Conversations with Nostradamus,
    Volume I, II, III
Jesus and the Essenes
They Walked with Jesus
Between Death and Life
A Soul Remembers Hiroshima
Keepers of the Garden.
The Legend of Starcrash
The Custodians
The Convoluted Universe - Book One,
    Two, Three, Four
Five Lives Remembered
The Three Waves of Volunteers and the
    New Earth
The Search for Hidden, Sacred
    Knowledge
Stuart Wilson & Joanna Prentis
The Essenes - Children of the Light
Power of the Magdalene
Beyond Limitations
Atlantis and the New Consciousness
The Magdalene Version
O.T. Bonnett, M.D./Greg Satre
Reincarnation: The View from Eternity
What I Learned After Medical School
Why Healing Happens
M. Don Schorn
Elder Gods of Antiquity
Legacy of the Elder Gods
Gardens of the Elder Gods
Reincarnation...Stepping Stones of Life
Aron Abrahamsen
Holiday in Heaven
Out of the Archives – Earth Changes
Sherri Cortland
Windows of Opportunity
Raising Our Vibrations for the New Age
The Spiritual Toolbox
Michael Dennis
Morning Coffee with God
God's Many Mansions
Nikki Pattillo
Children of the Stars
A Spiritual Evolution
Rev. Grant H. Pealer
Worlds Beyond Death
A Funny Thing Happened on the Way to
    Heaven
Maiya & Geoff Gray-Cobb
Angels - The Guardians of Your Destiny
Maiya Gray-Cobb
Seeds of the Soul
Sture Lönnerstrand
I Have Lived Before
Arun & Sunanda Gandhi
The Forgotten Woman

Claire Doyle Beland
Luck Doesn't Happen by Chance
James H. Kent
Past Life Memories As A Confederate
    Soldier
Dorothy Leon
Is Jehovah An E.T
Justine Alessi & M. E. McMillan
Rebirth of the Oracle
Donald L. Hicks
The Divinity Factor
Christine Ramos, RN
A Journey Into Being
Mary Letorney
Discover The Universe Within You
Debra Rayburn
Let's Get Natural With Herbs
Jodi Felice
The Enchanted Garden
Susan Mack & Natalia Krawetz
My Teachers Wear Fur Coats
Ronald Chapman
Seeing True
Rev. Keith Bender
The Despiritualized Church
Vara Humphreys
The Science of Knowledge
Karen Peebles
The Other Side of Suicide
Antoinette Lee Howard
Journey Through Fear
Julia Hanson
Awakening To Your Creation
Irene Lucas
Thirty Miracles in Thirty Days
Mandeep Khera
Why?
Robert Winterhalter
The Healing Christ
James Wawro
Ask Your Inner Voice
Tom Arbino
You Were Destined to be Together
Maureen McGill & Nola Davis
Live From the Other Side
Anita Holmes
TWIDDERS
Walter Pullen
Evolution of the Spirit
Cinnamon Crow
Teen Oracle
Chakra Zodiac Healing Oracle

For more information about any of the above titles, soon to be released titles,
or other items in our catalog, write or visit our website:
PO Box 754, Huntsville, AR 72740
www.ozarkmt.com

Other Books By Ozark Mountain Publishing, Inc.

For more information about any of the above titles, soon to be released titles,
or other items in our catalog, write or visit our website:
PO Box 754, Huntsville, AR 72740
www.ozarkmt.com